C. J. T.

Folk-lore and Legends

Scotland

C. J. T.

Folk-lore and Legends
Scotland

ISBN/EAN: 9783744773423

Printed in Europe, USA, Canada, Australia, Japan

Cover: Foto ©Thomas Meinert / pixelio.de

More available books at **www.hansebooks.com**

FOLK-LORE

AND

LEGENDS

SCOTLAND

W. W. GIBBINGS
18 BURY ST., LONDON, W.C.
1889

PREFATORY NOTE

THE distinctive features of Scotch Folklore are such as might have been expected from a consideration of the characteristics of Scotch scenery. The rugged grandeur of the mountain, the solemn influence of the widespreading moor, the dark face of the deep mountain loch, the babbling of the little stream, seem all to be reflected in the popular tales and superstitions. The acquaintance with nature in a severe, grand, and somewhat terrible form must necessarily have its effect on the human mind, and the Scotch mind and character bear the impress of their natural surroundings. The fairies, the brownies, the bogles of Scotland are the same beings as those with whom the Irish have peopled the hills, the nooks, and the streams of their land, yet how different, how distinguished from their counterparts, how clothed, as it were, in the national dress !

CONTENTS

CANOBIE DICK AND THOMAS OF ERCILDOUN.

Now it chanced many years since that there lived
on the Borders a jolly rattling horse-cowper, who
was remarkable for a reckless and fearless temper,
which made him much admired and a little dreaded
amongst his neighbours. One moonlight night, as
he rode over Bowden Moor, on the west side of the
Eildon Hills, the scene of Thomas the Rhymer's
prophecies, and often mentioned in his history,
having a brace of horses along with him, which he
had not been able to dispose of, he met a man of
venerable appearance and singularly antique dress,
who, to his great surprise, asked the price of his
horses, and began to chaffer with him on the subject.
To Canobie Dick, for so shall we call our Border
dealer, a chap was a chap, and he would have sold a
horse to the devil himself, without minding his
cloven hoof, and would have probably cheated Old
Nick into the bargain. The stranger paid the price
they agreed on, and all that puzzled Dick in the
transaction was, that the gold which he received was

Scotch.

A

in unicorns, bonnet-pieces, and other ancient coins, which would have been invaluable to collectors, but were rather troublesome in modern currency. It was gold, however, and therefore Dick contrived to get better value for the coin than he perhaps gave to his customer. By the command of so good a merchant, he brought horses to the same spot more than once; the purchaser only stipulating that he should always come by night and alone. I do not know whether it was from mere curiosity, or whether some hope of gain mixed with it, but after Dick had sold several horses in this way, he began to complain that dry bargains were unlucky, and to hint, that since his chap must live in the neighbourhood, he ought, in the courtesy of dealing, to treat him to half a mutchkin.

"You may see my dwelling if you will," said the stranger; "but if you lose courage at what you see there, you will rue it all your life."

Dickon, however, laughed the warning to scorn, and having alighted to secure his horse, he followed the stranger up a narrow footpath, which led them up the hills to the singular eminence stuck betwixt the most southern and the centre peaks, and called, from its resemblance to such an animal in its form, the Lucken Hare. At the foot of this eminence, which is almost as famous for witch-meetings as the neighbouring windmill of Kippilaw, Dick was somewhat startled to observe that his conductor entered the hillside by a passage or cavern, of which he himself, though well acquainted with the spot, had never seen nor heard.

"You may still return," said his guide, looking ominously back upon him; but Dick scorned to show the white feather, and on they went. They entered a very long range of stables; in every stall stood a coal-black horse; by every horse lay a knight in coal-black armour, with a drawn sword in his hand; but all were as silent, hoof and limb, as if they had been cut out of marble. A great number of torches lent a gloomy lustre to the hall, which, like those of the Caliph Vathek, was of large dimensions. At the upper end, however, they at length arrived, where a sword and horn lay on an antique table.

"He that shall sound that horn and draw that sword," said the stranger, who now intimated that he was the famous Thomas of Ercildoun, "shall, if his heart fail him not, be king over all broad Britain. So speaks the tongue that cannot lie. But all depends on courage, and much on your taking the sword or horn first."

Dick was much disposed to take the sword, but his bold spirit was quailed by the supernatural terrors of the hall, and he thought to unsheathe the sword first might be construed into defiance, and give offence to the powers of the mountain. He took the bugle with a trembling hand, and blew a feeble note, but loud enough to produce a terrible answer. Thunder rolled in stunning peals through the immense hall; horses and men started to life; the steeds snorted, stamped, ground their bits, and tossed their heads; the warriors sprang to their feet, clashed their armour, and brandished their swords. Dick's terror was extreme at seeing the whole army, which had been so lately silent as the grave, in uproar, and · about to rush on him. He dropped the horn, and made a feeble attempt to seize the enchanted sword; but at the same moment a voice pronounced aloud the mysterious words—

"Woe to the coward, that ever he was born,
Who did not draw the sword before he blew the horn!"

At the same time a whirlwind of irresistible fury howled through the long hall, bore the unfortunate horse-jockey clear out of the mouth of the cavern, and precipitated him over a steep bank of loose stones, where the shepherds found him the next morning, with just breath sufficient to tell his fearful tale, after concluding which he expired.

COINNACH OER.

Coinnach Oer, which means Dun Kenneth, was a celebrated man in his generation. He has been called the Isaiah of the North. The prophecies of this man are very frequently alluded to and quoted in various parts of the Highlands ; although little is known of the man himself, except in Ross-shire. He was a small farmer in Strathpeffer, near Ding-wall, and for many years of his life neither exhibited any talents, nor claimed any intelligence above his fellows. The manner in which he obtained the prophetic gift was told by himself in the following manner :—

As he was one day at work in the hill casting (digging) peats, he heard a voice which seemed to call to him out of the air. It commanded him to dig under a little green knoll which was near, and to gather up the small white stones which he would discover beneath the turf. The voice informed him, at the same time, that while he kept these stones in his possession, he should be endued with the power of supernatural foreknowledge.

5

Kenneth, though greatly alarmed at this aerial conversation, followed the directions of his invisible instructor, and turning up the turf on the hillock, in a little time discovered the talismans. From that day forward, the mind of Kenneth was illuminated by gleams of unearthly light; and he made many predictions, of which the credulity of the people, and the coincidence of accident, often supplied confirmation; and he certainly became the most notable of the Highland prophets. The most remarkable and well known of his vaticinations is the following:—"Whenever a M'Lean with long hands, a Fraser with a black spot on his face, a M'Gregor with a black knee, and a club-footed M'Leod of Raga, shall have existed; whenever there shall have been successively three M'Donalds of the name of John, and three M'Kinnons of the same Christian name,—oppressors will appear in the country, and the people will change their own land for a strange one." All these personages have appeared since; and it is the common opinion of the peasantry, that the consummation of the prophecy was fulfilled, when the exaction of the exorbitant rents reduced the Highlanders to poverty, and the introduction of the sheep banished the people to America.

Whatever might have been the gift of Kenneth Oer, he does not appear to have used it with an extraordinary degree of discretion; and the last time he exercised it, he was very near paying dear for his divination.

On this occasion he happened to be at some high festival of the M'Kenzies at Castle Braan. One of the guests was so exhilarated by the scene of gaiety, that he could not forbear an eulogium on the gallantry of the feast, and the nobleness of the guests. Kenneth, it appears, had no regard for the M'Kenzies, and was so provoked by this sally in their praise, that he not only broke out into a severe satire against their whole race, but gave vent to the prophetic denunciation of wrath and confusion upon their posterity. The guests being informed (or having overheard a part) of this rhapsody, instantly rose up with one accord to punish the contumely of the prophet. Kenneth, though he foretold the fate of others, did not in any manner look into that of himself; for this reason, being doubtful of debating the propriety of his prediction upon such unequal terms, he fled with the greatest precipitation. The M'Kenzies followed with infinite zeal; and more than one ball had whistled over the head of the seer before he reached Loch Ousie. The consequences of this prediction so disgusted Kenneth with any further exercise of his prophetic calling, that, in the anguish of his flight, he solemnly renounced all communication with its power; and, as he ran along the margin of Loch Ousie, he took out the wonderful pebbles, and cast them in a fury into the water. Whether his evil genius had now forsaken him, or his condition was better than that of his pursuers, is unknown, but certain it is, Kenneth, after the sacrifice of the pebbles, outstripped his enraged enemies, and never, so far as I have heard, made any attempt at prophecy from the hour of his escape.

Kenneth Oer had a son, who was called Ian Dubh Mac Coinnach (Black John, the son of Kenneth), and lived in the village of Miltoun, near Dingwall. His chief occupation was brewing whisky; and he was killed in a fray at Miltoun, early in the present century. His exit would not have formed the catastrophe of an epic poem, and appears to have been one of those events of which his father had no intelligence, for it happened in the following manner :—

Having fallen into a dispute with a man with whom he had previously been on friendly terms, they proceeded to blows; in the scuffle, the boy, the son of Ian's adversary, observing the two combatants locked in a close and firm gripe of eager contention, and being doubtful of the event, ran into the house and brought out the iron pot-crook, with which he saluted the head of the unfortunate Ian so severely, that he not only relinquished his combat, but departed this life on the ensuing morning.

ELPHIN IRVING,

THE FAIRIES' CUPBEARER.

" The lady kilted her kirtle green
    A little aboon her knee,
The lady snooded her yellow hair
    A little aboon her bree,
And she's gane to the good greenwood
    As fast as she could hie.

·And first she let the black steed pass,
    And syne she let the brown,
And then she flew to the milk-white steed,
    And pulled the rider down :
Syne out then sang the queen o' the fairies,
    Frae midst a bank of broom,
She that has won him, young Tamlane,
    Has gotten a gallant groom."
                                    Old Ballad.

"THE romantic vale of Corriewater, in Annandale,
is regarded by the inhabitants, a pastoral and un-
mingled people, as the last border refuge of those
beautiful and capricious beings, the fairies. Many
old people yet living imagine they have had intercourse of good words and good deeds with the 'good
folk'; and continue to tell that in the ancient

9

days the fairies danced on the hill, and revelled in the glen, and showed themselves, like the mysterious children of the deity of old, among the sons and daughters of men. Their visits to the earth were periods of joy and mirth to mankind, rather than of sorrow and apprehension. They played on musical instruments of wonderful sweetness and variety of note, spread unexpected feasts, the supernatural flavour of which overpowered on many occasions the religious scruples of the Presbyterian shepherds, performed wonderful deeds of horsemanship, and marched in midnight processions, when the sound of their elfin minstrelsy charmed youths and maidens into love for their persons and pursuits; and more than one family of Corriewater have the fame of augmenting the numbers of the elfin chivalry. Faces of friends and relatives, long since doomed to the battle-trench or the deep sea, have been recognised by those who dared to gaze on the fairy march. The maid has seen her lost lover, and the mother her stolen child; and the courage to plan and achieve their deliverance has been possessed by, at least, one border maiden. In the legends of the people of Corrievale, there is a singular mixture of elfin and human adventure, and the traditional story of the Cupbearer to the Queen of the Fairies appeals alike to our domestic feelings and imagination.

"In one of the little green loops or bends on the banks of Corriewater, mouldered walls, and a few stunted wild plum-trees and vagrant roses, still point out the site of a cottage and garden. A well of pure spring-water leaps out from an old tree-root before the door; and here the shepherds, shading themselves in summer from the influence of the sun, tell to their children the wild tale of Elphin Irving and his sister Phemie; and, singular as the story seems, it has gained full credence among the people where the scene is laid."

"I ken the tale and the place weel," interrupted an old Scottish woman, who, from the predominance of scarlet in her apparel, seemed to have been a follower of the camp,—"I ken them weel, and the tale's as true as a bullet to its aim and a spark to powder. O bonnie Corriewater, a thousand times have I pulled gowans on its banks wi' ane that lies stiff and stark on a foreign shore in a bloody grave;" and, sobbing audibly, she drew the remains of a military cloak over her face, and allowed the story to proceed.

"When Elphin Irving and his sister Phemie were in their sixteenth year, for tradition says they were twins, their father was drowned in Corriewater, attempting to save his sheep from a sudden swell, to which all mountain streams are liable; and their mother, on the day of her husband's burial, laid down her head on the pillow, from which, on the seventh day, it was lifted to be dressed for the same grave. The inheritance left to the orphans may be

briefly described : seventeen acres of plough and
pasture land, seven milk cows, and seven pet sheep
(many old people take delight in odd numbers);
and to this may be added seven bonnet-pieces of
Scottish gold, and a broadsword and spear, which
their ancestor had wielded with such strength and
courage in the battle of Dryfe Sands, that the
minstrel who sang of that deed of arms ranked him
only second to the Scotts and Johnstones.

"The youth and his sister grew in stature and in
beauty.   The brent bright brow, the clear blue eye,
and frank and blithe deportment of the former gave
him some influence among the young women of the
valley ; while the latter was no less the admiration
of the young men, and at fair and dance, and at
bridal, happy was he who touched but her hand, or
received the benediction of her eye.   Like all other
Scottish beauties, she was the theme of many a
song ; and while tradition is yet busy with the
singular history of her brother, song has taken all
the care that rustic minstrelsy can of the gentleness
of her spirit and the charms of her person."

"Now I vow," exclaimed a wandering piper, "by
mine own honoured instrument, and by all other
instruments that ever yielded music for the joy and
delight of mankind, that there are more bonnie songs
made about fair Phemie Irving than about all other
dames of Annandale, and many of them are both high
and bonnie.   A proud lass maun she be if her spirit

hears; and men say the dust lies not insensible of beautiful verse; for her charms are breathed through a thousand sweet lips, and no further gone than yestermorn I heard a lass singing on a green hill-side what I shall not readily forget. If ye like to listen, ye shall judge; and it will not stay the story long, nor mar it much, for it is short, and about Phemie Irving." And, accordingly, he chanted the following rude verses, not unaccompanied by his honoured instrument, as he called his pipe, which chimed in with great effect, and gave richness to a voice which felt better than it could express :—

FAIR PHEMIE IRVING.

Gay is thy glen, Corrie,
   With all thy groves flowering;
Green is thy glen, Corrie,
   When July is showering;
And sweet is yon wood where
   The small birds are bowering,
And there dwells the sweet one
   Whom I am adoring.

Her round neck is whiter
   Than winter when snowing;
Her meek voice is milder
   Than Ae in its flowing;
The glad ground yields music
   Where she goes by the river;
One kind glance would charm me
   For ever and ever.

The proud and the wealthy
   To Phemie are bowing;
No looks of love win they
   With sighing or suing;

Far away maun I stand
    With my rude wooing,
She's a flow'ret too lovely
    Too bloom for my pu'ing.

Oh were I yon violet
    On which she is walking ;
Oh were I yon small bird
    To which she is talking ;
Or yon rose in her hand,
    With its ripe ruddy blossom ;
Or some pure gentle thought
    To be blest with her bosom.

This minstrel interruption, while it established
Phemie Irving's claim to grace and to beauty, gave
me additional confidence to pursue the story.

"But minstrel skill and true love-tale seemed to
want their usual influence when they sought to win
her attention ; she was only observed to pay most
respect to those youths who were most beloved by
her brother ; and the same hour that brought these
twins to the world seemed to have breathed through
them a sweetness and an affection of heart and
mind which nothing could divide. If, like the
virgin queen of the immortal poet, she walked ' in
maiden meditation fancy free,' her brother Elphin
seemed alike untouched with the charms of the
fairest virgins in Corrie. He ploughed his field, he
reaped his grain, he leaped, he ran, and wrestled,
and danced, and sang, with more skill and life and
grace than all other youths of the district ; but he
had no twilight and stolen interviews ; when all

other young men had their loves by their side, he was single, though not unsought, and his joy seemed never perfect save when his sister was near him. If he loved to share his time with her, she loved to share her time with him alone, or with the beasts of the field, or the birds of the air. She watched her little flock late, and she tended it early; not for the sordid love of the fleece, unless it was to make mantles for her brother, but with the look of one who had joy in its company. The very wild creatures, the deer and the hares, seldom sought to shun her approach, and the bird forsook not its nest, nor stinted its song, when she drew nigh; such is the confidence which maiden innocence and beauty inspire.

"It happened one summer, about three years after they became orphans, that rain had been for a while withheld from the earth, the hillsides began to parch, the grass in the vales to wither, and the stream of Corrie was diminished between its banks to the size of an ordinary rill. The shepherds drove their flocks to moorlands, and marsh and tarn had their reeds invaded by the scythe to supply the cattle with food. The sheep of his sister were Elphin's constant care; he drove them to the moistest pastures during the day, and he often watched them at midnight, when flocks, tempted by the sweet dewy grass, are known to browse eagerly, that he might guard them from the fox, and lead

them to the choicest herbage. In these nocturnal
watchings he sometimes drove his little flock over
the water of Corrie, for the fords were hardly ankle-
deep; or permitted his sheep to cool themselves in
the stream, and taste the grass which grew along
the brink. All this time not a drop of rain fell,
nor did a cloud appear in the sky.

"One evening, during her brother's absence with
the flock, Phemie sat at her cottage-door, listening
to the bleatings of the distant folds and the lessened
murmur of the water of Corrie, now scarcely audible
beyond its banks. Her eyes, weary with watching
along the accustomed line of road for the return of
Elphin, were turned on the pool beside her, in
which the stars were glimmering fitful and faint.
As she looked she imagined the water grew brighter
and brighter; a wild illumination presently shone
upon the pool, and leaped from bank to bank, and
suddenly changing into a human form, ascended
the margin, and, passing her, glided swiftly into the
cottage. The visionary form was so like her brother
in shape and air, that, starting up, she flew into the
house, with the hope of finding him in his customary
seat. She found him not, and, impressed with the
terror which a wraith or apparition seldom fails to
inspire, she uttered a shriek so loud and so piercing
as to be heard at Johnstone Bank, on the other
side of the vale of Corrie."

An old woman now rose suddenly from her seat

in the window-sill, the living dread of shepherds, for she travelled the country with a brilliant reputation for witchcraft, and thus she broke in upon the narrative : " I vow, young man, ye tell us the truth upset and down-thrust. I heard my douce grandmother say that on the night when Elphin Irving disappeared—disappeared I shall call it, for the bairn can but be gone for a season, to return to us in his own appointed time—she was seated at the fireside at Johnstone Bank ; the laird had laid aside his bonnet to take the Book, when a shriek mair loud, believe me, than a mere woman's shriek—and they can shriek loud enough, else they're sair wranged— came over the water of Corrie, so sharp and shrilling, that the pewter plates dinneled on the wall ; such a shriek, my douce grandmother said, as rang in her ear till the hour of her death, and she lived till she was aughty-and-aught, forty full ripe years after the event. But there is another matter, which, doubtless, I cannot compel ye to believe : it was the common rumour that Elphin Irving came not into the world like the other sinful creatures of the earth, but was one of the kane-bairns of the fairies, whilk they had to pay to the enemy of man's salvation every seventh year. The poor lady-fairy—a mother's aye a mother, be she elves' flesh or Eve's flesh—hid her elf son beside the christened flesh in Marion Irving's cradle, and the auld enemy lost his prey for a time. Now, hasten on with your story,

Scotch.

which is not a bodle the waur for me. The maiden
saw the shape of her brother, fell into a faint, or a
trance, and the neighbours came flocking in—gang
on with your tale, young man, and dinna be
affronted because an auld woman helped ye wi 't."

"It is hardly known," I resumed, "how long
Phemie Irving continued in a state of insensibility.
The morning was far advanced, when a neighbouring maiden found her seated in an old chair, as
white as monumental marble; her hair, about which
she had always been solicitous, loosened from its
curls, and hanging disordered over her neck and
bosom, her hands and forehead. The maiden
touched the one, and kissed the other; they were
as cold as snow; and her eyes, wide open, were
fixed on her brother's empty chair, with the intensity of gaze of one who had witnessed the appearance of a spirit. She seemed insensible of any
one's presence, and sat fixed and still and motionless. The maiden, alarmed at her looks, thus
addressed her :—' Phemie, lass, Phemie Irving!
Dear me, but this be awful! I have come to tell
ye that seven of your pet sheep have escaped drowning in the water; for Corrie, sae quiet and sae
gentle yestreen, is rolling and dashing frae bank to
bank this morning. Dear me, woman, dinna let the
loss of the world's gear bereave ye of your senses.
I would rather make ye a present of a dozen mug-
ewes of the Tinwald brood myself; and now I think

on 't, if ye 'll send over Elphin, I will help him
hame with them in the gloaming myself. So,
Phemie, woman, be comforted.'

"At the mention of her brother's name she cried
out, 'Where is he? Oh, where is he?' gazed wildly
round, and, shuddering from head to foot, fell sense-
less on the floor. Other inhabitants of the valley,
alarmed by the sudden swell of the river, which
had augmented to a torrent, deep and impassable,
now came in to inquire if any loss had been sus-
tained, for numbers of sheep and teds of hay had
been observed floating down about the dawn of the
morning. They assisted in reclaiming the unhappy
maiden from her swoon; but insensibility was joy
compared to the sorrow to which she awakened.
'They have ta'en him away, they have ta'en him
away,' she chanted, in a tone of delirious pathos;
'him that was whiter and fairer than the lily on
Lyddal Lee. They have long sought, and they have
long sued, and they had the power to prevail against
my prayers at last. They have ta'en him away;
the flower is plucked from among the weeds, and
the dove is slain amid a flock of ravens. They came
with shout, and they came with song, and they
spread the charm, and they placed the spell, and
the baptised brow has been bowed down to the
unbaptised hand. They have ta'en him away, they
have ta'en him away; he was too lovely, and too
good, and too noble, to bless us with his continuance

on earth ; for what are the sons of men compared
to him ?—the light of the moonbeam to the morning sun, the glowworm to the eastern star. They
have ta'en him away, the invisible dwellers of the
earth. I saw them come on him with shouting and
with singing, and they charmed him where he sat,
and away they bore him ; and the horse he rode
was never shod with iron, nor owned before the
mastery of human hand. They have ta'en him
away over the water, and over the wood, and over
the hill. I got but ae look of his bonnie blue ee,
but ae, ae look. But as I have endured what never
maiden endured, so will I undertake what never
maiden undertook, I will win him from them all.
I know the invisible ones of the earth ; I have
heard their wild and wondrous music in the wild
woods, and there shall a christened maiden seek
him, and achieve his deliverance.' She paused, and
glancing around a circle of condoling faces, down
which the tears were dropping like rain, said, in a
calm and altered but still delirious tone : 'Why do
you weep, Mary Halliday ? and why do you weep,
John Graeme ? Ye think that Elphin Irving—oh,
it 's a bonnie, bonnie name, and dear to many a
maiden's heart as well as mine—ye think he is
drowned in Corrie ; and ye will seek in the deep,
deep pools for the bonnie, bonnie corse, that ye may
weep over it, as it lies in its last linen, and lay it,
amid weeping and wailing in the dowie kirkyard.

Ye may seek, but ye shall never find; so leave me
to trim up my hair, and prepare my dwelling, and
make myself ready to watch for the hour of his return to upper earth.' And she resumed her household labours with an alacrity which lessened not the
sorrow of her friends.

"Meanwhile the rumour flew over the vale that
Elphin Irving was drowned in Corriewater. Matron
and maid, old man and young, collected suddenly
along the banks of the river, which now began to
subside to its natural summer limits, and commenced
their search ; interrupted every now and then by
calling from side to side, and from pool to pool, and
by exclamations of sorrow for this misfortune. The
search was fruitless : five sheep, pertaining to the
flock which he conducted to pasture, were found
drowned in one of the deep eddies ; but the river
was still too brown, from the soil of its moorland
sources, to enable them to see what its deep shelves,
its pools, and its overhanging and hazelly banks
concealed. They remitted further search till the
stream should become pure ; and old man taking
old man aside, began to whisper about the mystery
of the youth's disappearance; old women laid their
lips to the ears of their coevals, and talked of
Elphin Irving's fairy parentage, and his having been
dropped by an unearthly hand into a Christian
cradle. The young men and maids conversed on
other themes ; they grieved for the loss of the

friend and the lover, and while the former thought that a heart so kind and true was not left in the vale, the latter thought, as maidens will, on his handsome person, gentle manners, and merry blue eye, and speculated with a sigh on the time when they might have hoped a return for their love. They were soon joined by others who had heard the wild and delirious language of his sister : the old belief was added to the new assurance, and both again commented upon by minds full of superstitious feeling, and hearts full of supernatural fears, till the youths and maidens of Corrievale held no more love trysts for seven days and nights, lest, like Elphin Irving, they should be carried away to augment the ranks of the unchristened chivalry.

" It was curious to listen to the speculations of the peasantry. 'For my part,' said a youth, 'if I were sure that poor Elphin escaped from that perilous water, I would not give the fairies a pound of hiplock wool for their chance of him. There has not been a fairy seen in the land since Donald Cargil, the Cameronian, conjured them into the Solway for playing on their pipes during one of his nocturnal preachings on the hip of the Burnswark hill.'

" ' Preserve me, bairn,' said an old woman, justly exasperated at the incredulity of her nephew, 'if ye winna believe what I both heard and saw at the moonlight end of Craigyburnwood on a summer night, rank after rank of the fairy folk, ye 'll at least believe a douce man and a ghostly professor, even the late minister of Tinwaldkirk. His only son—I mind the lad weel, with his long yellow locks and his bonnie blue eyes—when I was but a gilpie of a lassie, *he* was stolen away from off the horse at his father's elbow, as they crossed that false and fearsome water, even Locherbriggflow, on the night of the Midsummer fair of Dumfries. Ay, ay, who can doubt the truth of that? Have not the godly inhabitants of Almsfieldtown and Tinwaldkirk seen the sweet youth riding at midnight, in the midst of the unhallowed troop, to the sound of flute and of dulcimer, and though meikle they prayed, naebody tried to achieve his deliverance?'

" ' I have heard it said by douce folk and sponsible,' interrupted another, ' that every seven years the elves and fairies pay kane, or make an offering of one of their children, to the grand enemy of salvation, and that they are permitted to purloin one of the children of men to present to the fiend—a more acceptable offering, I 'll warrant, than one of their own infernal brood that are Satan's sib allies, and drink a drop of the deil's blood every May morning. And touching this lost lad, ye all ken his mother was a hawk of an uncanny nest, a second cousin of Kate Kimmer, of Barfloshan, as rank a witch as ever rode on ragwort. Ay, sirs, what 's bred in the bone is ill to come out of the flesh.'

" On these and similar topics, which a peasantry
full of ancient tradition and enthusiasm and superstition readily associate with the commonest occurrences of life, the people of Corrievale continued to
converse till the fall of evening, when each, seeking
their home, renewed again the wondrous subject,
and illustrated it with all that popular belief and
poetic imagination could so abundantly supply.

" The night which followed this melancholy day
was wild with wind and rain ; the river came down
broader and deeper than before, and the lightning,
flashing by fits over the green woods of Corrie,
showed the ungovernable and perilous flood sweeping above its banks. It happened that a farmer,
returning from one of the border fairs, encountered
the full swing of the storm ; but mounted on an
excellent horse, and mantled from chin to heel in a
good grey plaid, beneath which he had the further
security of a thick greatcoat, he sat dry in his saddle,
and proceeded in the anticipated joy of a subsided
tempest and a glowing morning sun. As he entered
the long grove, or rather remains of the old Galwegian
forest, which lines for some space the banks of the
Corriewater, the storm began to abate, the wind
sighed milder and milder among the trees, and here
and there a star, twinkling momentarily through
the sudden rack of the clouds, showed the river
raging from bank to brae. As he shook the moisture
from his clothes, he was not without a wish that the

day would dawn, and that he might be preserved on a road which his imagination beset with greater perils than the raging river; for his superstitious feeling let loose upon his path elf and goblin, and the current traditions of the district supplied very largely to his apprehension the ready materials of fear.

" Just as he emerged from the wood, where a fine sloping bank, covered with short greensward, skirts the limit of the forest, his horse made a full pause, snorted, trembled, and started from side to side, stooped his head, erected his ears, and seemed to scrutinise every tree and bush. The rider, too, it may be imagined, gazed round and round, and peered warily into every suspicious-looking place. His dread of a supernatural visitation was not much allayed when he observed a female shape seated on the ground at the root of a huge old oak-tree, which stood in the centre of one of those patches of verdant sward, known by the name of 'fairy rings,' and avoided by all peasants who wish to prosper. A long thin gleam of eastern daylight enabled him to examine accurately the being who, in this wild place and unusual hour, gave additional terror to this haunted spot. She was dressed in white from the neck to the knees; her arms, long and round and white, were perfectly bare; her head, uncovered, allowed her long hair to descend in ringlet succeeding ringlet, till the half of her person was nearly concealed in the fleece. Amidst the whole, her hands were constantly busy in shedding aside the tresses which interposed between her steady and uninterrupted gaze down a line of old road which wound among the hills to an ancient burial-ground.

"As the traveller continued to gaze, the figure suddenly rose, and, wringing the rain from her long locks, paced round and round the tree, chanting in a wild and melancholy manner an equally wild and delirious song.

THE FAIRY OAK OF CORRIEWATER.

The small bird's head is under its wing,
   The deer sleeps on the grass ;
The moon comes out, and the stars shine down,
   The dew gleams like the glass :
There is no sound in the world so wide,
   Save the sound of the smitten brass,
With the merry cittern and the pipe
   Of the fairies as they pass.
But oh ! the fire maun burn and burn,
And the hour is gone, and will never return.

The green hill cleaves, and forth, with a bound,
   Comes elf and elfin steed ;
The moon dives down in a golden cloud,
   The stars grow dim with dread ;
But a light is running along the earth,
   So of heaven's they have no need :
O'er moor and moss with a shout they pass,
   And the word is spur and speed—
But the fire maun burn, and I maun quake,
And the hour is gone that will never come back.

And when they came to Craigyburnwood,
  The Queen of the Fairies spoke :
" Come, bind your steeds to the rushes so green,
  And dance by the haunted oak :
I found the acorn on Heshbon Hill,
  In the nook of a palmer's poke,
A thousand years since ; here it grows ! "
And they danced till the greenwood shook :
But oh ! the fire, the burning fire,
The longer it burns, it but blazes the higher.

" I have won me a youth," the Elf Queen said,
  " The fairest that earth may see ;
This night I have won young Elph Irving
  My cupbearer to be.
His service lasts but seven sweet years,
  And his wage is a kiss of me."
And merrily, merrily, laughed the wild elves
  Round Corris's greenwood tree.
But oh ! the fire it glows in my brain,
And the hour is gone, and comes not again.

The Queen she has whispered a secret word,
  " Come hither my Elphin sweet,
And bring that cup of the charméd wine,
  Thy lips and mine to weet."
But a brown elf shouted a loud, loud shout,
  " Come, leap on your coursers fleet,
For here comes the smell of some baptised flesh,
  And the sounding of baptised feet."
But oh ! the fire that burns, and maun burn ;
For the time that is gone will never return.

On a steed as white as the new-milked milk,
  The Elf Queen leaped with a bound,
And young Elphin a steed like December snow
  'Neath him at the word he found.
But a maiden came, and her christened arms
  She linked her brother around,

And called on God, and the steed with a snort
  Sank into the gaping ground.
But the fire maun burn, and I maun quake,
And the time that is gone will no more come back.

And she held her brother, and lo ! he grew
  A wild bull waked in ire ;
And she held her brother, and lo ! he changed
  To a river roaring higher ;
And she held her brother, and he became
  A flood of the raging fire ;
She shrieked and sank, and the wild elves laughed
  Till the mountain rang and mire.
But oh ! the fire yet burns in my brain,
And the hour is gone, and comes not again.

" O maiden, why waxed thy faith so faint,
  Thy spirit so slack and slaw ?
Thy courage kept good till the flame waxed wud,
  Then thy might begun to thaw ;
Had ye kissed him with thy christened lip,
  Ye had wan him frae 'mang us a'.
Now bless the fire, the elfin fire,
  That made thee faint and fa' ;
Now bless the fire, the elfin fire,
The longer it burns it blazes the higher."

" At the close of this unusual strain, the figure
sat down on the grass, and proceeded to bind up
her long and disordered tresses, gazing along the
old and unfrequented road. 'Now God be my
helper,' said the traveller, who happened to be the
laird of Johnstone Bank, 'can this be a trick of the
fiend, or can it be bonnie Phemie Irving who chants
this dolorous sang ? Something sad has befallen
that makes her seek her seat in this eerie nook
amid the darkness and tempest ; through might from

aboon I will go on and see.' And the horse, feeling something of the owner's reviving spirit in the application of spur-steel, bore him at once to the foot of the tree. The poor delirious maiden uttered a yell of piercing joy as she beheld him, and, with the swiftness of a creature winged, linked her arms round the rider's waist, and shrieked till the woods rang. ' Oh, I have ye now, Elphin, I have ye now,' and she strained him to her bosom with a convulsive grasp. ' What ails ye, my bonnie lass?' said the laird of Johnstone Bank, his fears of the supernatural vanishing when he beheld her sad and bewildered look. She raised her eyes at the sound, and seeing a strange face, her arms slipped their hold, and she dropped with a groan on the ground.

"The morning had now fairly broke; the flocks shook the rain from their sides, the shepherds hastened to inspect their charges, and a thin blue smoke began to stream from the cottages of the valley into the brightening air. The laird carried Phemie Irving in his arms, till he observed two shepherds ascending from one of the loops of Corriewater, bearing the lifeless body of her brother. They had found him whirling round and round in one of the numerous eddies, and his hands, clutched and filled with wool, showed that he had lost his life in attempting to save the flock of his sister. A plaid was laid over the body, which, along with the unhappy maiden in a half-lifeless state, was carried into a cottage, and laid in that apartment distinguished among the peasantry by the name of the chamber. While the peasant's wife was left to take care of Phemie, old man and matron and maid had collected around the drowned youth, and each began to relate the circumstances of his death, when the door suddenly opened, and his sister, advancing to the corpse, with a look of delirious serenity, broke out into a wild laugh and said : 'Oh, it is wonderful, it's truly wonderful ! That bare and death-cold body, dragged from the darkest pool of Corrie, with its hands filled with fine wool, wears the perfect similitude of my own Elphin ! I'll tell ye—the spiritual dwellers of the earth, the fairyfolk of our evening tale, have stolen the living body, and fashioned this cold and inanimate clod to mislead your pursuit. In common eyes this seems all that Elphin Irving would be, had he sunk in Corriewater ; but so it seems not to me. Ye have sought the living soul, and ye have found only its garment. But oh, if ye had beheld him, as I beheld him to-night, riding among the elfin troop, the fairest of them all ; had you clasped him in your arms, and wrestled for him with spirits and terrible shapes from the other world, till your heart quailed and your flesh was subdued, then would ye yield no credit to the semblance which this cold and apparent flesh bears to my brother. But hearken ! On Hallowmass Eve, when the spiritual people are let loose on earth for a season, I will take my stand in the burial-ground of Corrie; and when my Elphin and his unchristened troop come past, with the sound of all their minstrelsy, I will leap on him and win him, or perish for ever.'

"All gazed aghast on the delirious maiden, and many of her auditors gave more credence to her distempered speech than to the visible evidence before them. As she turned to depart, she looked round, and suddenly sank upon the body, with tears streaming from her eyes, and sobbed out, "My brother! Oh, my brother!' She was carried out insensible, and again recovered; but relapsed into her ordinary delirium, in which she continued till the Hallow Eve after her brother's burial. She was found seated in the ancient burial-ground, her back against a broken gravestone, her locks white with frost-rime, watching with intensity of look the road to the kirkyard; but the spirit which gave life to the fairest form of all the maids of Annandale was fled for ever."

Such is the singular story which the peasants know by the name of "Elphin Irving, the Fairies' Cupbearer"; and the title, in its fullest and most supernatural sense, still obtains credence among the industrious and virtuous dames of the romantic vale of Corrie.

THE GHOSTS OF CRAIG-AULNAIC.

Two celebrated ghosts existed, once on a time, in the wilds of Craig-Aulnaic, a romantic place in the district of Strathdown, Banffshire. The one was a male and the other a female. The male was called Fhuna Mhoir Ben Baynac, after one of the mountains of Glenavon, where at one time he resided; and the female was called Clashnichd Aulnaic, from her having had her abode in Craig-Aulnaic. But although the great ghost of Ben Baynac was bound by the common ties of nature and of honour to protect and cherish his weaker companion, Clashnichd Aulnaic, yet he often treated her in the most cruel and unfeeling manner. In the dead of night, when the surrounding hamlets were buried in deep repose, and when nothing else disturbed the solemn stillness of the midnight scene, oft would the shrill shrieks of poor Clashnichd burst upon the slumberer's ears, and awake him to anything but pleasant reflections.

But of all those who were incommoded by the noisy and unseemly quarrels of these two ghosts, James Owre or Gray, the tenant of the farm of

Balbig of Delnabo, was the greatest sufferer. From the proximity of his abode to their haunts, it was the misfortune of himself and family to be the nightly audience of Clashnichd's cries and lamentations, which they considered anything but agreeable entertainment.

One day as James Gray was on his rounds looking after his sheep, he happened to fall in with Clashnichd, the ghost of Aulnaic, with whom he entered into a long conversation. In the course of it he took occasion to remonstrate with her on the very disagreeable disturbance she caused himself and family by her wild and unearthly cries—cries which, he said, few mortals could relish in the dreary hours of midnight. Poor Clashnichd, by way of apology for her conduct, gave James Gray a sad account of her usage, detailing at full length the series of cruelties committed upon her by Ben Baynac. From this account, it appeared that her living with the latter was by no means a matter of choice with Clashnichd; on the contrary, it seemed that she had, for a long time, lived apart with much comfort, residing in a snug dwelling, as already mentioned, in the wilds of Craig-Aulnaic; but Ben Baynac having unfortunately taken into his head to pay her a visit, took a fancy, not to herself, but her dwelling, of which, in his own name and authority, he took immediate possession, and soon after he expelled poor Clashnichd, with many stripes, from her natural

Scotch.

C

inheritance. Not satisfied with invading and de-
priving her of her just rights, he was in the habit of
following her into her private haunts, not with the
view of offering her any endearments, but for the
purpose of inflicting on her person every torment
which his brain could invent.

Such a moving relation could not fail to affect the
generous heart of James Gray, who determined from
that moment to risk life and limb in order to vindi-
cate the rights and avenge the wrongs of poor
Clashnichd, the ghost of Craig-Aulnaic. He, therefore, took good care to interrogate his new *protégée*
touching the nature of her oppressor's constitution,
whether he was of that *killable* species of ghost that
could be shot with a silver sixpence, or if there was
any other weapon that could possibly accomplish his
annihilation. Clashnichd informed him that she had
occasion to know that Ben Baynac was wholly
invulnerable to all the weapons of man, with the
exception of a large mole on his left breast, which
was no doubt penetrable by silver or steel; but
that, from the specimens she had of his personal
prowess and strength, it were vain for mere
man to attempt to combat him. Confiding, however, in his expertness as an archer—for he was
allowed to be the best marksman of the age—
James Gray told Clashnichd he did not fear him
with all his might,—that *he* was a man; and
desired her, moreover, next time the ghost chose

to repeat his incivilities to her, to apply to him,
James Gray, for redress.

It was not long ere he had an opportunity of ful-
filling his promises.   Ben Baynac having one night,
in the want of better amusement, entertained himself
by inflicting an inhuman castigation on Clashnichd,
she lost no time in waiting on James Gray, with a
full and particular account of it.   She found him
smoking his *cutty*, for it was night when she came to
him; but, notwithstanding the inconvenience of the
hour, James needed no great persuasion to induce
him to proceed directly along with Clashnichd to
hold a communing with their friend, Ben Baynac,
the great ghost.   Clashnichd was stout and sturdy,
and understood the knack of travelling much better
than our women do.   She expressed a wish that,
for the sake of expedition, James Gray would suffer
her to bear him along, a motion to which the latter
agreed; and a few minutes brought them close to
the scene of Ben Baynac's residence.   As they
approached his haunt, he came forth to meet them,
with looks and gestures which did not at all indicate
a cordial welcome.   It was a fine moonlight night, and
they could easily observe his actions.   Poor Clashnichd was now sorely afraid of the great ghost.
Apprehending instant destruction from his fury, she
exclaimed to James Gray that they would be both
dead people, and that immediately, unless James
Gray hit with an arrow the mole which covered Ben

Baynac's heart. This was not so difficult a task as James had hitherto apprehended it. The mole was as large as a common bonnet, and yet nowise disproportioned to the natural size of the ghost's body, for he certainly was a great and a mighty ghost. Ben Baynac cried out to James Gray that he would soon make eagle's meat of him; and certain it is, such was his intention, had not the shepherd so effectually stopped him from the execution of it. Raising his bow to his eye when within a few yards of Ben Baynac, he took deliberate aim; the arrow flew—it hit—a yell from Ben Baynac announced the result. A hideous howl re-echoed from the surrounding mountains, responsive to the groans of a thousand ghosts; and Ben Baynac, like the smoke of a shot, vanished into air.

Clashnichd, the ghost of Aulnaic, now found herself emancipated from the most abject state of slavery, and restored to freedom and liberty, through the invincible courage of James Gray. Overpowered with gratitude, she fell at his feet, and vowed to devote the whole of her time and talents towards his service and prosperity. Meanwhile, being anxious to have her remaining goods and furniture removed to her former dwelling, whence she had been so iniquitously expelled by Ben Baynac, the great ghost, she requested of her new master the use of his horses to remove them. James observing on the adjacent hill a flock of deer, and wishing to have a trial of his new servant's sagacity or expertness, told her those were his horses—she was welcome to the use of them; desiring that when she had done with them, she would inclose them in his stable. Clash-nichd then proceeded to make use of the horses, and James Gray returned home to enjoy his night's rest.

Scarce had he reached his arm-chair, and reclined his cheek on his hand, to ruminate over the bold adventure of the night, when Clashnichd entered, with her "breath in her throat," and venting the bitterest complaints at the unruliness of his horses, which had broken one-half of her furniture, and caused her more trouble in the stabling of them than their services were worth.

"Oh! they are stabled, then?" inquired James Gray. Clashnichd replied in the affirmative. "Very well," rejoined James, "they shall be tame enough to-morrow."

From this specimen of Clashnichd, the ghost of Craig-Aulnaic's expertness, it will be seen what a valuable acquisition her service proved to James Gray and his young family. They were, however, speedily deprived of her assistance by a most un-fortunate accident. From the sequel of the story, from which the foregoing is an extract, it appears that poor Clashnichd was deeply addicted to propen-sities which at that time rendered her kin so obnoxious to their human neighbours. She was constantly in the habit of visiting her friends much oftener than she was invited, and, in the course of such visits, was never very scrupulous in making free with any eatables which fell within the circle of her observation.

One day, while engaged on a foraging expedition of this description, she happened to enter the Mill of Delnabo, which was inhabited in those days by the miller's family. She found his wife engaged in roasting a large gridiron of fine savoury fish, the agreeable smell proceeding from which perhaps occasioned her visit. With the usual inquiries after the health of the miller and his family, Clash-nichd proceeded with the greatest familiarity and good-humour to make herself comfortable at their expense. But the miller's wife, enraged at the loss of her fish, and not relishing such unwelcome familiarity, punished the unfortunate Clashnichd rather too severely for her freedom. It happened that there was at the time a large caldron of boiling water suspended over the fire, and this caldron the enraged wife overturned in Clashnichd's bosom!

Scalded beyond recovery, she fled up the wilds of Craig-Aulnaic, uttering the most melancholy lamentations, nor has she been ever heard of since.

THE DOOMED RIDER.

"THE Conan is as bonny a river as we hae in a' the north country. There's mony a sweet sunny spot on its banks, an' mony a time an' aft hae I waded through its shallows, whan a boy, to set my little scautling-line for the trouts an' the eels, or to gather the big pearl-mussels that lie sae thick in the fords. But its bonny wooded banks are places for enjoying the day in—no for passing the nicht. I kenna how it is; it's nane o' your wild streams that wander desolate through a desert country, like the Aven, or that come rushing down in foam and thunder, ower broken rocks, like the Foyers, or that wallow in darkness, deep, deep in the bowels o' the earth, like the fearfu' Auldgraunt; an' yet no ane o' these rivers has mair or frightfuller stories connected wi' it than the Conan. Ane can hardly saunter ower half-a-mile in its course, frae where it leaves Coutin till where it enters the sea, without passing ower the scene o' some frightful auld legend o' the kelpie or the waterwraith. And ane o' the most frightful looking o' these places is to be found among the woods of Conan House. Ye enter a swampy meadow that waves wi' flags an' rushes like a corn-field in harvest, an' see a hillock covered wi' willows rising like an island in the midst. There are thick mirk-woods on ilka side; the river, dark an' awesome, an' whirling round an' round in mossy eddies, sweeps away behind it; an' there is an auld burying-ground, wi' the broken ruins o' an auld Papist kirk, on the tap. Ane can see amang the rougher stanes the rose-wrought mullions of an arched window, an' the trough that ance held the holy water. About twa hunder years ago—a wee mair maybe, or a wee less, for ane canna be very sure o' the date o' thae old stories—the building was entire; an' a spot near it, whar the wood now grows thickest, was laid out in a corn-field. The marks o' the furrows may still be seen amang the trees.

" A party o' Highlanders were busily engaged, ae day in harvest, in cutting down the corn o' that field; an' just aboot noon, when the sun shone brightest an' they were busiest in the work, they heard a voice frae the river exclaim :—' The hour but not the man has come.' Sure enough, on look-ing round, there was the kelpie stan'in' in what they ca' a fause ford, just fornent the auld kirk. There is a deep black pool baith aboon an' below, but i' the ford there's a bonny ripple, that shows, as ane might think, but little depth o' water; an' just i'

the middle o' that, in a place where a horse might
swim, stood the kelpie. An' it again repeated its
words :—'The hour but not the man has come,' an'
then flashing through the water like a drake, it disappeared in the lower pool. When the folk stood
wondering what the creature might mean, they saw
a man on horseback come spurring down the hill in
hot haste, making straight for the fause ford. They
could then understand her words at ance ; an' four
o' the stoutest o' them sprang oot frae amang the
corn to warn him o' his danger, an' keep him back.
An' sae they tauld him what they had seen an'
heard, an' urged him either to turn back an' tak'
anither road, or stay for an hour or sae where he
was. But he just wadna hear them, for he was
baith unbelieving an' in haste, an' wauld hae taen
the ford for a' they could say, hadna the Highlanders, determined on saving him whether he would
or no, gathered round him an' pulled him frae his
horse, an' then, to mak' sure o' him, locked him up
in the auld kirk. Weel, when the hour had gone
by—the fatal hour o' the kelpie—they flung open
the door, an' cried to him that he might noo gang
on his journey. Ah! but there was nae answer,
though ; an' sae they cried a second time, an' there
was nae answer still; an' then they went in,
an' found him lying stiff an' cauld on the floor,
wi' his face buried in the water o' the very stone
trough that we may still see amang the ruins.

His hour had come, an' he had fallen in a
fit, as 'twould seem, head - foremost amang the
water o' the trough, where he had been smothered,
—an' sae ye see, the prophecy o' the kelpie availed
naething."

WHIPPETY STOURIE.

THERE was once a gentleman that lived in a very grand house, and he married a young lady that had been delicately brought up. In her husband's house she found everything that was fine—fine tables and chairs, fine looking-glasses, and fine curtains; but then her husband expected her to be able to spin twelve hanks o' thread every day, besides attending to her house; and, to tell the even-down truth, the lady could not spin a bit. This made her husband glunchy with her, and, before a month had passed, she found hersel' very unhappy.

One day the husband gaed away upon a journey, after telling her that he expected her, before his return, to have not only learned to spin, but to have spun a hundred hanks o' thread. Quite downcast, she took a walk along the hillside, till she cam' to a big flat stane, and there she sat down and grat. By and by she heard a strain o' fine sma' music, coming as it were frae aneath the stane, and, on turning it up, she saw a cave below, where there were sitting

six wee ladies in green gowns, ilk ane o' them
spinning on a little wheel, and singing,

> " Little kens my dame at hame
> That Whippety Stourie is my name."

The lady walked into the cave, and was kindly
asked by the wee bodies to take a chair and sit
down, while they still continued their spinning.
She observed that ilk ane's mouth was thrawn away
to ae side, but she didna venture to speer the reason.
They asked why she looked so unhappy, and she
telt them that it was she was expected by her husband to be a good spinner, when the plain truth was
that she could not spin at all, and found herself
quite unable for it, having been so delicately brought
up ; neither was there any need for it, as her husband was a rich man.

" Oh, is that a' ?" said the little wifies, speaking
out of their cheeks alike.

" Yes, and is it not a very good a' too ?" said the
lady, her heart like to burst wi' distress.

." We could easily quit ye o' that trouble," said
the wee women. " Just ask us a' to dinner for the
day when your husband is to come back. We 'll
then let you see how we 'll manage him."

So the lady asked them all to dine with herself
and her husband, on the day when he was to come
back.

When the gudeman came hame, he found the

house so occupied with preparations for dinner, that he had nae time to ask his wife about her thread; and, before ever he had ance spoken to her on the subject, the company was announced at the hall door. The six ladies all came in a coach-and-six, and were as fine as princesses, but still wore their gowns of green. The gentleman was very polite, and showed them up the stair with a pair of wax candles in his hand. And so they all sat down to dinner, and conversation went on very pleasantly, till at length the husband, becoming familiar with them, said—

"Ladies, if it be not an uncivil question, I should like to know how it happens that all your mouths are turned away to one side?"

"Oh," said ilk ane at ance, "it's with our constant *spin-spin-spinning.*"

"Is that the case?" cried the gentleman; "then, John, Tam, and Dick, fie, go haste and burn every rock, and reel, and spinning-wheel in the house, for I'll not have my wife to spoil her bonnie face with *spin-spin-spinning.*"

And so the lady lived happily with her gudeman all the rest of her days.

THE WEIRD OF THE THREE ARROWS.

SIR JAMES DOUGLAS, the companion of Bruce, and well known by his appellation of the "Black Douglas," was once, during the hottest period of the exterminating war carried on by him and his colleague Randolph, against the English, stationed at Linthaughlee, near Jedburgh. He was resting, himself and his men after the toils of many days' fighting-marches through Teviotdale; and, according to his custom, had walked round the tents, previous to retiring to the unquiet rest of a soldier's bed. He stood for a few minutes at the entrance to his tent contemplating the scene before him, rendered more interesting by a clear moon, whose silver beams fell, in the silence of a night without a breath of wind, calmly on the slumbers of mortals destined to mix in the melée of dreadful war, perhaps on the morrow. As he stood gazing, irresolute whether to retire to rest or indulge longer in a train of thought not very suitable to a warrior who delighted in the spirit-stirring scenes of his profession, his eye was attracted by the figure of an old woman, who ap-

proached him with a trembling step, leaning on a
staff, and holding in her left hand three English
cloth-shaft arrows.

"You are he who is ca'ed the guid Sir James?"
said the old woman.

"I am, good woman," replied Sir James.   "Why
hast thou wandered from the sutler's camp?"

"I dinna belang to the camp o' the hoblers,"
answered the woman.   "I hae been a residenter in
Linthaughlee since the day when King Alexander
passed the door o' my cottage wi' his bonny French
bride, wha was terrified awa' frae Jedburgh by the
death's-head whilk appeared to her on the day o'
her marriage.   What I hae suffered sin' that day"
(looking at the arrows in her hand) "lies between
me an' heaven."

"Some of your sons have been killed in the wars,
I presume?" said Sir James.

"Ye hae guessed a pairt o' my waes," replied the
woman.   "That arrow" (holding out one of the
three) "carries on its point the bluid o' my first
born; that is stained wi' the stream that poured
frae the heart o' my second; and that is red wi' the
gore in which my youngest weltered, as he gae up
the life that made me childless.   They were a' shot
by English hands, in different armies, in different
battles.   I am an honest woman, and wish to return
to the English what belongs to the English; but
that in the same fashion in which they were sent.

The Black Douglas has the strongest arm an' the surest ee in auld Scotland; an' wha can execute my commission better than he?"

"I do not use the bow, good woman," replied Sir James. "I love the grasp of the dagger or the battle-axe. You must apply to some other individual to return your arrows."

"I canna tak' them hame again," said the woman, laying them down at the feet of Sir James. "Ye'll see me again on St. James' E'en."

The old woman departed as she said these words. Sir James took up the arrows, and placed them in an empty quiver that lay amongst his baggage. He retired to rest, but not to sleep. The figure of the old woman and her strange request occupied his thoughts, and produced trains of meditation which ended in nothing but restlessness and disquietude. Getting up at daybreak, he met a messenger at the entrance of his tent, who informed him that Sir Thomas de Richmont, with a force of ten thousand men, had crossed the Borders, and would pass through a narrow defile, which he mentioned, where he could be attacked with great advantage. Sir James gave instant orders to march to the spot; and, with that genius for scheming, for which he was so remarkable, commanded his men to twist together the young birch-trees on either side of the passage to prevent the escape of the enemy. This finished, he concealed his archers in a hollow way, near the gorge of the pass.

The enemy came on; and when their ranks were embarrassed by the narrowness of the road, and it was impossible for the cavalry to act with effect, Sir James rushed upon them at the head of his horsemen; and the archers, suddenly discovering themselves, poured in a flight of arrows on the confused soldiers, and put the whole army to flight. In the heat of the onset, Douglas killed Sir Thomas de Richmont with his dagger.

Not long after this, Edmund de Cailon, a knight of Gascony, and Governor of Berwick, who had been heard to vaunt that he had sought the famous Black Knight, but could not find him, was returning to England, loaded with plunder, the fruit of an inroad on Teviotdale. Sir James thought it a pity that a Gascon's vaunt should be heard unpunished in Scotland, and made long forced marches to satisfy the desire of the foreign knight, by giving him a sight of the dark countenance he had made a subject of reproach. He soon succeeded in gratifying both himself and the Gascon. Coming up in his terrible manner, he called to Cailon to stop, and, before he proceeded into England, receive the respects of the Black Knight he had come to find, but hitherto had not met. The Gascon's vaunt was now changed; but shame supplied the place of courage, and he ordered his men to receive Douglas's attack. Sir James assiduously sought his enemy. He at last succeeded; and a single combat ensued,

of a most desperate character. But who ever
escaped the arm of Douglas when fairly opposed to
him in single conflict? Cailon was killed; he had
met the Black Knight at last.

"So much," cried Sir James, "for the vaunt of a
Gascon!"

Similar in every respect to the fate of Cailon, was
that of Sir Ralph Neville. He, too, on hearing the
great fame of Douglas's prowess, from some of
Cailon's fugitive soldiers, openly boasted that he
would fight with the Scottish Knight, if he would
come and show his banner before Berwick. Sir
James heard the boast and rejoiced in it. He
marched to that town, and caused his men to ravage
the country in front of the battlements, and burn
the villages. Neville left Berwick with a strong
body of men; and, stationing himself on a high
ground, waited till the rest of the Scots should
disperse to plunder; but Douglas called in his
detachment and attacked the knight. After a desperate conflict, in which many were slain, Douglas,
as was his custom, succeeded in bringing the leader
to a personal encounter, and the skill of the Scottish
knight was again successful. Neville was slain, and
his men utterly discomfited.

Having retired one night to his tent to take
some rest after so much pain and toil, Sir James
Douglas was surprised by the reappearance of the
old woman whom he had seen at Linthaughlee.

"This is the feast o' St. James," said she, as she approached him. "I said I would see ye again this nicht, an' I'm as guid's my word. Hae ye returned the arrows I left wi' ye to the English wha sent them to the hearts o' my sons?"

"No," replied Sir James. "I told ye I did not fight with the bow. Wherefore do ye importune me thus?"

"Give me back the arrows then," said the woman.

Sir James went to bring the quiver in which he had placed them. On taking them out, he was surprised to find that they were all broken through the middle.

"How has this happened?" said he. "I put these arrows in this quiver entire, and now they are broken."

"The weird is fulfilled!" cried the old woman, laughing eldrichly, and clapping her hands. "That broken shaft cam' frae a soldier o' Richmont's; that frae ane o' Cailon's, and that frae ane o' Neville's. They are a' dead, an' I am revenged!"

The old woman then departed, scattering, as she went, the broken fragments of the arrows on the floor of the tent.

THE LAIRD OF BALMACHIE'S WIFE.

In the olden times, when it was the fashion for gentlemen to wear swords, the Laird of Balmachie went one day to Dundee, leaving his wife at home ill in bed. Riding home in the twilight, he had occasion to leave the high road, and when crossing between some little romantic knolls, called the Curhills, in the neighbourhood of Carlungy, he encountered a troop of fairies supporting a kind of litter, upon which some person seemed to be borne. Being a man of dauntless courage, and, as he said, impelled by some internal impulse, he pushed his horse close to the litter, drew his sword, laid it across the vehicle, and in a firm tone exclaimed—

"In the name of God, release your captive."

The tiny troop immediately disappeared, dropping the litter on the ground. The laird dismounted, and found that it contained his own wife, dressed in her bedclothes. Wrapping his coat around her, he placed her on the horse before him, and, having only a short distance to ride, arrived safely at home.

Placing her in another room, under the care of an attentive friend, he immediately went to the chamber where he had left his wife in the morning, and there to all appearance she still lay, very sick of a fever. She was fretful, discontented, and complained much of having been neglected in his absence, at all of which the laird affected great concern, and pretending much sympathy, insisted upon her rising to have her bed made. She said that she was unable to rise, but her husband was peremptory, and having ordered a large wood fire to warm the room, he lifted the impostor from the bed, and bearing her across the floor as if to a chair, which had been previously prepared, he threw her on the fire, from which she bounced like a sky-rocket, and went through the ceiling, and out at the roof of the house, leaving a hole among the slates. He then brought in his own wife, a little recovered from her alarm, who said, that sometime after sunset, the nurse having left her for the purpose of preparing a little candle, a multitude of elves came in at the window, thronging like bees from a hive. They filled the room, and having lifted her from the bed carried her through the window, after which she recollected nothing further, till she saw her husband standing over her on the Cur-hills, at the back of

Carlungy. The hole in the roof, by which the female fairy made her escape, was mended, but could never be kept in repair, as a tempest of wind happened always once a year, which uncovered that particular spot, without injuring any other part of the roof.

MICHAEL SCOTT.

In the early part of Michael Scott's life he was in the habit of emigrating annually to the Scottish metropolis, for the purpose of being employed in his capacity of mason. One time as he and two companions were journeying to the place of their destination for a similar object, they had occasion to pass over a high hill, the name of which is not men-' tioned, but which is supposed to have been one of the Grampians, and being fatigued with climbing, they sat down to rest themselves. They had no sooner done so than they were warned to take to their heels by the hissing of a large serpent, which they observed revolving itself towards them with great velocity. Terrified at the sight, Michael's two companions fled, while he, on the contrary, resolved to encounter the reptile. The appalling monster approached Michael Scott with distended mouth and forked tongue; and, throwing itself into a coil at his feet, was raising its head to inflict a mortal sting, when Michael, with one stroke of his stick, severed its body into three pieces. Having rejoined his affrighted comrades, they resumed their journey; and, on arriving at the next public-house, it being late, and the travellers being weary, they took up their quarters at it for the night. In the course of the night's conversation, reference was naturally made to Michael's recent exploit with the serpent, when the landlady of the house, who was remarkable for her " arts," happened to be present. Her curiosity appeared much excited by the conversation ; and, after making some inquiries regarding the colour of the serpent, which she was told was white, she offered any of them that would procure her the middle piece such a tempting reward, as induced one of the party instantly to go for it. The distance was not very great ; and on reaching the spot, he found the middle and tail piece in the place where Michael left them, but the head piece was gone

The landlady on receiving the piece, which still vibrated with life, seemed highly gratified at her acquisition ; and, over and above the promised reward, regaled her lodgers very plentifully with the choicest dainties in her house. Fired with curiosity to know the purpose for which the serpent was intended, the wily Michael Scott was immediately seized with a severe fit of indisposition, which caused him to prefer the request that he might be allowed to sleep beside the fire, the warmth of which, he affirmed, was in the highest degree beneficial to him.

Never suspecting Michael Scott's hypocrisy, and naturally supposing that a person so severely indisposed would feel very little curiosity about the contents of any cooking utensils which might lie around the fire, the landlady allowed his request. As soon as the other inmates of the house were retired to bed, the landlady resorted to her darling occupation ; and, in his feigned state of indisposition, Michael had a favourable opportunity of watching most scrupulously all her actions through the keyhole of a door leading to the next apartment where she was. He could see the rites and ceremonies with which the serpent was put into the oven, along with many mysterious ingredients. After which the unsuspicious landlady placed the dish by the fireside, where lay the distressed traveller, to stove till the morning.

Once or twice in the course of the night the " wife of the change-house," under the pretence of inquiring for her sick lodger, and administering to him some renovating cordials, the beneficial effects of which he gratefully acknowledged, took occasion to dip her finger in her saucepan, upon which the cock, perched on his roost, crowed aloud. All Michael's sickness could not prevent him considering very inquisitively the landlady's cantrips, and particularly the influence of the sauce upon the crowing of the cock. Nor could he dissipate some inward desires he felt to follow her example. At the same time, he suspected that Satan had a hand in the pie, yet he thought he would like very much to be at the bottom of the concern ; and thus his reason and his curiosity clashed against each other for the space of several hours. At length passion, as is too often the case, became the conqueror. Michael, too, dipped his finger in the sauce, and applied it to the tip of his tongue, and immediately the cock perched on the *spardan* announced the circumstance in a mournful clarion. Instantly his mind received a new light to which he was formerly a stranger, and the astonished dupe of a landlady now found it her interest to admit her sagacious lodger into a knowledge of the remainder of her secrets.

Endowed with the knowledge of "good and evil," and all the "second sights" that can be acquired, Michael left his lodgings in the morning, with the philosopher's stone in his pocket. By daily perfecting his supernatural attainments, by new series of discoveries, he became more than a match for Satan himself. Having seduced some thousands of Satan's best workmen into his employment, he trained them up so successfully to the architective business, and inspired them with such industrious habits, that he was more than sufficient for all the architectural work of the empire. To establish this assertion, we need only refer to some remains of his workmanship still existing north of the Grampians, some of them, stupendous bridges built by him in one short night, with no other visible agents than two or three workmen.

On one occasion work was getting scarce, as might have been naturally expected, and his workmen, as they were wont, flocked to his doors, perpetually exclaiming, "Work! work! work!" Continually annoyed by their incessant entreaties, he called out to them in derision to go and make a dry road from Fortrose to Arderseir, over the Moray Firth. Immediately their cry ceased, and as Scott supposed it wholly impossible for them to execute his order, he retired to rest, laughing most heartily at the chimerical sort of employment he had given to his industrious workmen. Early in the morning, however, he got up and took a walk at the break of day down to the shore to divert himself at the fruitless labours of his zealous workmen. But on reaching the spot, what was his astonishment to find the formidable piece of work allotted to them only a few hours before already nearly finished. Seeing the great damage the commercial class of the community would sustain from the operation, he ordered the workmen to demolish the most part of their work; leaving, however, the point of Fortrose to show the traveller to this day the wonderful exploit of Michael Scott's fairies.

On being thus again thrown out of employment, their former clamour was resumed, nor could Michael Scott, with all his sagacity, devise a plan to keep

them in innocent employment. He at length discovered one. "Go," says he, "and manufacture
me ropes that will carry me to the back of the
moon, of these materials—*miller's-sudds* and sea-sand."
Michael Scott here obtained rest from his active
operators; for, when other work failed them, he
always despatched them to their rope manufactory.
But though these agents could never make proper
ropes of those materials, their efforts to that effect
are far from being contemptible, for some of their
ropes are seen by the sea-side to this day.

We shall close our notice of Michael Scott by
reciting one anecdote of him in the latter part of his
life.

In consequence of a violent quarrel which Michael
Scott once had with a person whom he conceived to
have caused him some injury, he resolved, as the
highest punishment he could inflict upon him, to
send his adversary to that evil place designed only
for Satan and his black companions. He accordingly, by means of his supernatural machinations,
sent the poor unfortunate man thither; and had he
been sent by any other means than those of Michael
Scott, he would no doubt have met with a warm
reception. Out of pure spite to Michael, however,
when Satan learned who was his billet-master, he
would no more receive him than he would receive
the Wife of Beth; and instead of treating the
unfortunate man with the harshness characteristic

of him, he showed him considerable civilities. In-
troducing him to his "Ben Taigh," he directed her
to show the stranger any curiosities he might wish
to see, hinting very significantly that he had provided some accommodation for their mutual friend,
Michael Scott, the sight of which might afford him
some gratification. The polite housekeeper accordingly conducted the stranger through the principal
apartments in the house, where he saw fearful sights.
But the bed of Michael Scott!—his greatest enemy
could not but feel satiated with revenge at the sight
of it. It was a place too horrid to be described,
filled promiscuously with all the awful brutes ima-
ginable. Toads and lions, lizards and leeches, and,
amongst the rest, not the least conspicuous, a large
serpent gaping for Michael Scott, with its mouth
wide open. This last sight having satisfied the
stranger's curiosity, he was led to the outer gate,
and came away. He reached his friends, and, among
other pieces of news touching his travels, he was
not backward in relating the entertainment that
awaited his friend Michael Scott, as soon as he
would "stretch his foot" for the other world. But
Michael did not at all appear disconcerted at his
friend's intelligence. He affirmed that he would
disappoint all his enemies in their expectations—in
proof of which he gave the following signs : "When
I am just dead," says he, "open my breast and
extract my heart. Carry it to some place where

the public may see the result. You will then transfix it upon a long pole, and if Satan will have my soul, he will come in the likeness of a black raven and carry it off; and if my soul will be saved it will be carried off by a white dove."

His friends faithfully obeyed his instructions. Having exhibited his heart in the manner directed, a large black raven was observed to come from the east with great fleetness, while a white dove came from the west with equal velocity. The raven made a furious dash at the heart, missing which, it was unable to curb its force, till it was considerably past it; and the dove, reaching the spot at the same time, carried off the heart amidst the rejoicing and ejaculations of the spectators.

THE MINISTER AND THE FAIRY.

NOT long since, a pious clergyman was returning home, after administering spiritual consolation to a dying member of his flock. It was late of the night, and he had to pass through a good deal of *uncanny* land. He was, however, a good and a conscientious minister of the Gospel, and feared not all the spirits in the country. On his reaching the end of a lake which stretched along the roadside for some distance, he was a good deal surprised at hearing the most melodious strains of music. Overcome by pleasure and curiosity, the minister coolly sat down to listen to the harmonious sounds, and try what new dis-coveries he could make with regard to their nature and source. He had not sat many minutes before he could distinguish the approach of the music, and also observe a light in the direction from whence it proceeded gliding across the lake towards him. In-stead of taking to his heels, as any faithless wight would have done, the pastor fearlessly determined to await the issue of the phenomenon. As the light and music drew near, the clergyman could at

length distinguish an object resembling a human
being walking on the surface of the water, attended
by a group of diminutive musicians, some of them
bearing lights, and others instruments of music,
from which they continued to evoke those melodious
strains which first attracted his attention. The
leader of the band dismissed his attendants, landed
on the beach, and afforded the minister the amplest opportunities of examining his appearance.
He was a little primitive-looking grey-headed man,
clad in the most grotesque habit the clergyman had
ever seen, and such as led him at once to suspect
his real character. He walked up to the minister,
whom he saluted with great grace, offering an
apology for his intrusion. The pastor returned his
compliments, and, without further explanation, invited the mysterious stranger to sit down by his
side. The invitation was complied with, upon which
the minister proposed the following question :—
"Who art thou, stranger, and from whence ?"

To this question the fairy, with downcast eye,
replied that he was one of those sometimes called
Doane Shee, or men of peace, or good men, though
the reverse of this title was a more fit appellation
for them. Originally angelic in his nature and
attributes, and once a sharer of the indescribable
joys of the regions of light, he was seduced by Satan
to join him in his mad conspiracies ; and, as a
punishment for his transgression, he was cast down

from those regions of bliss, and was now doomed, along with millions of fellow-sufferers, to wander through seas and mountains, until the coming of the Great Day. What their fate would be then they could not divine, but they apprehended the worst. "And," continued he, turning to the minister, with great anxiety, "the object of my present intrusion on you is to learn your opinion, as an eminent divine, as to our final condition on that dreadful day."

Here the venerable pastor entered upon a long conversation with the fairy, touching the principles of faith and repentance. Receiving rather unsatisfactory answers to his questions, the minister desired the "sheech" to repeat after him the Paternoster, in attempting to do which, it was not a little remarkable that he could not repeat the word "art," but said "*wert*," in heaven. Inferring from every circumstance that their fate was extremely precarious, the minister resolved not to puff the fairies up with presumptuous, and, perhaps, groundless expectations. Accordingly, addressing himself to the unhappy fairy, who was all anxiety to know the nature of his sentiments, the reverend gentleman told him that he could not take it upon him to give them any hopes of pardon, as their crime was of so deep a hue as scarcely to admit of it. On this the unhappy fairy uttered a shriek of despair, plunged headlong into the loch, and the minister resumed his course to his home.

Scotch.

E

THE FISHERMAN AND THE MERMAN.

OF mermen and merwomen many strange stories
are told in the Shetland Isles. Beneath the depths
of the ocean, according to these stories, an atmosphere exists adapted to the respiratory organs of
certain beings, resembling, in form, the human race,
possessed of surpassing beauty, of limited supernatural powers, and liable to the incident of death.
They dwell in a wide territory of the globe, far
below the region of fishes, over which the sea, like
the cloudy canopy of our sky, loftily rolls, and they
possess habitations constructed of the pearl and coral
productions of the ocean. Having lungs not adapted
to a watery medium, but to the nature of atmo-
spheric air, it would be impossible for them to pass
through the volume of waters that intervenes between
the submarine and supramarine world, if it were
not for the extraordinary power they inherit of
entering the skin of some animal capable of existing in the sea, which they are enabled to occupy by
a sort of demoniacal possession. One shape they
put on, is that of an animal human above the waist,

yet terminating below in the tail and fins of a fish, but the most favourite form is that of the larger seal or Haaf-fish; for, in possessing an amphibious nature, they are enabled not only to exist in the ocean, but to land on some rock, where they frequently lighten themselves of their sea-dress, resume their proper shape, and with much curiosity examine the nature of the upper world belonging to the human race. Unfortunately, however, each merman or merwoman possesses but one skin, enabling the individual to ascend the seas, and if, on visiting the abode of man, the garb be lost, the hapless being must unavoidably become an inhabitant of the earth.

A story is told of a boat's crew who landed for the purpose of attacking the seals lying in the hollows of the crags at one of the stacks. The men stunned a number of the animals, and while they were in this state stripped them of their skins, with the fat attached to them. Leaving the carcasses on the rock, the crew were about to set off for the shore of Papa Stour, when such a tremendous swell arose that every one flew quickly to the boat. All succeeded in entering it except one man, who had imprudently lingered behind. The crew were unwilling to leave a companion to perish on the skerries, but the surge increased so fast, that after many unsuccessful attempts to bring the boat close in to the stack the unfortunate wight was left to his fate. A stormy night came on, and the deserted

Shetlander saw no prospect before him but that of perishing from cold and hunger, or of being washed into the sea by the breakers which threatened to dash over the rocks. At length, he perceived many of the seals, who, in their flight had escaped the attack of the boatmen, approach the skerry, disrobe themselves of their amphibious hides, and resume the shape of the sons and daughters of the ocean. Their first object was to assist in the recovery of their friends, who having been stunned by clubs, had, while in that state, been deprived of their skins. When the flayed animals had regained their sensibility, they assumed their proper form of mermen or merwomen, and began to lament in a mournful lay, wildly accompanied by the storm that was raging around, the loss of their sea-dress, which would prevent them from again enjoying their native azure atmosphere, and coral mansions that lay below the deep waters of the Atlantic. But their chief lamentation was for Ollavitinus, the son of Gioga, who, having been stripped of his seal's skin, would be for ever parted from his mates, and condemned to become an outcast inhabitant of the upper world. Their song was at length broken off, by observing one of their enemies viewing, with shivering limbs and looks of comfortless despair, the wild waves that dashed over the stack. Gioga immediately conceived the idea of rendering subservient to the advantage of the son the perilous situation of the man.

She addressed him with mildness, proposing to carry
him safe on her back across the sea to Papa Stour,
on condition of receiving the seal-skin of Ollavitinus.
A bargain was struck, and Gioga clad herself in her
amphibious garb; but the Shetlander, alarmed at
the sight of the stormy main that he was to ride
through, prudently begged leave of the matron, for
his better preservation, that he might be allowed to
cut a few holes in her shoulders and flanks, in order
to procure, between the skin and the flesh, a better
fastening for his hands and feet.   The request being
complied with, the man grasped the neck of the
seal, and committing himself to her care, she landed
him safely at Acres Gio in Papa Stour ; from which
place he immediately repaired to a skeo at Hamna
Voe, where the skin was deposited, and honourably
fulfilled his part of the contract, by affording Gioga
the means whereby her son could again revisit the
ethereal space over which the sea spread its green
mantle.

THE LAIRD O' CO'.

In the days of yore, the proprietors of Colzean, in Ayrshire (ancestors of the Marquis of Ailsa), were known in that country by the title of Lairds o' Co', a name bestowed on Colzean from some co's (or coves) in the rock beneath the castle.

One morning, a very little boy, carrying a small wooden can, addressed the Laird near the castle gate, begging for a little ale for his mother, who was sick. The Laird directed him to go to the butler and get his can filled; so away he went as ordered. The butler had a barrel of ale on tap, but about half full, out of which he proceeded to fill the boy's can; but to his extreme surprise he emptied the cask, and still the little can was not nearly full. The butler was unwilling to broach another barrel, but the little fellow insisted on the fulfilment of the Laird's order, and a reference was made to the Laird by the butler, who stated the miraculous capacity of the tiny can, and received instant orders to fill it if all the ale in the cellar would suffice. Obedient to this command, he broached another cask, but had scarcely drawn a drop when the can was full, and the dwarf departed with expressions of gratitude.

Some years afterwards the Laird being at the wars in Flanders was taken prisoner, and for some reason or other (probably as a spy) condemned to die a felon's death. The night prior to the day for his execution, being confined in a dungeon strongly barricaded, the doors suddenly flew open, and the dwarf reappeared, saying—

> " Laird o' Co',
> Rise an' go."

a summons too welcome to require repetition.

On emerging from prison, the boy caused him to mount on his shoulders, and in a short time set him down at his own gate, on the very spot where they had formerly met, saying—

> " Ae gude turn deserves anither—
> Tak' ye that for being sae kin' to my auld mither,"

and vanished.

EWEN OF THE LITTLE HEAD.

ABOUT three hundred years ago, Ewen Maclaine of Lochbuy, in the island of Mull, having been engaged in a quarrel with a neighbouring chief, a day was fixed for determining the affair by the sword. Lochbuy, before the day arrived, consulted a celebrated witch as to the result of the feud. The witch declared that if Lochbuy's wife should on the morning of that day give him and his men food unasked, he would be victorious, but if not, the result would be the reverse. This was a disheartening response for the unhappy votary, his wife being a noted shrew.

The fatal morning arrived, and the hour for meeting the enemy approached, but there appeared no symptoms of refreshment for Lochbuy and his men. At length the unfortunate man was compelled to ask his wife to supply them with food. She set down before them curds, but without spoons. When the husband inquired how they were to eat them, she replied they should assume the bills of hens. The men ate the curds, as well as they could, with their hands; but Lochbuy himself ate none. After

72

behaving with the greatest bravery in the bloody conflict which ensued, he fell covered with wounds, leaving his wife to the execration of the people. She is still known in that district under the appellation of Corr-dhu, or the Black Crane.

But the miseries brought on the luckless Lochbuy by his wife did not end with his life, for he died fasting, and his ghost is frequently seen to this day riding the very horse on which he was mounted when he was killed. It was a small, but very neat and active pony, dun or mouse-coloured, to which the Laird was much attached, and on which he had ridden for many years before his death. Its appearance is as accurately described in the island of Mull as any steed is at Newmarket. The prints of its shoes are discerned by connoisseurs, and the rattling of its curb is recognised in the darkest night. It is not particular with regard to roads, for it goes up hill and down dale with equal velocity. Its hard-fated rider still wears the same green cloak which covered him in his last battle; and he is particularly distinguished by the small size of his head, a peculiarity which, we suspect, the learned disciples of Spurzheim have never yet had the sagacity to discover as indicative of an extraordinary talent and incomparable perseverance in horsemanship.

It is now above three hundred years since Ewen-a-chin-vig (*Anglice*, Hugh of the Little Head) fell in the field of honour; but neither the vigour of the

horse nor of the rider is yet diminished. His
mournful duty has always been to attend the dying
moments of every member of his own tribe, and to
escort the departed spirit on its long and arduous
journey. He has been seen in the remotest of the
Hebrides; and he has found his way to Ireland on
these occasions long before steam navigation was
invented. About a century ago he took a fancy for
a young man of his own race, and frequently did
him the honour of placing him behind himself on
horseback. He entered into conversation with him,
and foretold many circumstances connected with the
fate of his successors, which have undoubtedly since
come to pass.

Many a long winter night have I listened to the
feats of Ewen-a-chin-vig, the faithful and indefatig-
able guardian of his ancient family, in the hour of
their last and greatest trial, affording an example
worthy the imitation of every chief,—perhaps not
beneath the notice of Glengarry himself.

About a dozen years since some symptoms of
Ewen's decay gave very general alarm to his friends.
He accosted one of his own people (indeed he never
has been known to notice any other), and, shaking
him cordially by the hand, he attempted to place
him on the saddle behind him, but the uncourteous
dog declined the honour. Ewen struggled hard,
but the clown was a great, strong, clumsy fellow,
and stuck to the earth with all his might. He

candidly acknowledged, however, that his chief would have prevailed, had it not been for a birch-tree which stood by, and which he got within the fold of his left arm. The contest became very warm indeed, and the tree was certainly twisted like an osier, as thousands can testify who saw it as well as myself. At length, however, Ewen lost his seat for the first time, and the instant the pony found he was his own master, he set off with the fleetness of lightning. Ewen immediately pursued his steed, and the wearied rustic sped his way homeward. It was the general opinion that Ewen found consider-able difficulty in catching the horse; but I am happy to learn that he has been lately seen riding the old mouse-coloured pony without the least change in either the horse or the rider. Long may he continue to do so!

Those who from motives of piety or curiosity have visited the sacred island of Iona, must remem-ber to have seen the guide point out the tomb of Ewen, with his figure on horseback, very elegantly sculptured in alto-relievo, and many of the above facts are on such occasions related.

JOCK AND HIS MOTHER.

YE see, there was a wife had a son, and they called him Jock; and she said to him, "You are a lazy fellow; ye maun gang awa' and do something for to help me." "Weel," says Jock, "I'll do that." So awa' he gangs, and fa's in wi' a packman. Says the packman, "If you carry my pack a' day, I'll gie you a needle at night." So he carried the pack, and got the needle; and as he was gaun awa' hame to his mither, he cuts a burden o' brackens, and put the needle into the heart o' them. Awa' he gaes hame. Says his mither, "What hae ye made o' yoursel' the day?" Says Jock, "I fell in wi' a packman, and carried his pack a' day, and he gae me a needle for't, and ye may look for it amang the brackens." "Hout," quo' she, "ye daft gowk, you should hae stuck it into your bonnet, man." "I'll mind that again," quo' Jock.

Next day he fell in wi' a man carrying plough socks. "If ye help me to carry my socks a' day, I'll gie ye ane to yersel' at night." "I'll do that," quo' Jock. Jock carried them a' day, and got a

sock, which he stuck in his bonnet. On the way
hame, Jock was dry, and gaed away to take a drink
out o' the burn; and wi' the weight o' the sock, his
bonnet fell into the river, and gaed out o' sight.
He gaed hame, and his mither says, "Weel, Jock,
what hae you been doing a' day?" And then he
tells her. "Hout," quo' she, "you should hae tied
the string to it, and trailed it behind you." "Weel,"
quo' Jock, "I'll mind that again."

Awa' he sets, and he fa's in wi' a flesher. "Weel,"
says the flesher, "if ye'll be my servant a' day, I'll
gie ye a leg o' mutton at night." "I'll be that,"
quo' Jock. He got a leg o' mutton at night. He
ties a string to it, and trails it behind him the hale
road hame. "What hae ye been doing?" said his
mither. He tells her. "Hout, you fool, ye should
hae carried it on your shouther." "I'll mind that
again," quo' Jock.

Awa' he gaes next day, and meets a horse-dealer.
He says, "If you will help me wi' my horses a' day,
I'll give you ane to yoursel' at night." "I'll do
that," quo' Jock. So he served him, and got his
horse, and he ties its feet; but as he was not able to
carry it on his back, he left it lying on the roadside.
Hame he comes, and tells his mither. "Hout, ye
daft gowk, ye'll ne'er turn wise! Could ye no hae
loupen on it, and ridden it?" "I'll mind that
again," quo' Jock.

Aweel, there was a grand gentleman, wha had a

daughter wha was very subject to melancholy; and
her father gae out that whaever should mak' her
laugh would get her in marriage. So it happened
that she was sitting at the window ae day, musing
in her melancholy state, when Jock, according to the
advice o' his mither, cam' flying up on a cow's back,
wi' the tail over his shouther. And she burst out
into a fit o' laughter. When they made inquiry
wha made her laugh, it was found to be Jock riding
on the cow. Accordingly, Jock was sent for to get
his bride. Weel, Jock was married to her, and
there was a great supper prepared. Amongst the
rest o' the things, there was some honey, which Jock
was very fond o'. After supper, they all retired,
and the auld priest that married them sat up a'
night by the kitchen fireside. So Jock waukens in
the night-time, and says, "Oh, wad ye gie me some
o' yon nice sweet honey that we got to our supper
last night?" "Oh ay," says his wife, "rise and
gang into the press, and ye'll get a pig fou o't."
Jock rose, and thrust his hand into the honey-pig for
a nievefu' o't, and he could not get it out. So he cam'
awa' wi' the pig in his hand, like a mason's mell,
and says, "Oh, I canna get my hand out." "Hoot,"
quo' she, "gang awa' and break it on the cheek-
stane." By this time, the fire was dark, and the
auld priest was lying snoring wi' his head against the
chimney-piece, wi' a huge white wig on. Jock gaes
awa', and gae him a whack wi' the honey-pig on the

head, thinking it was the cheek-stane, and knocks it a' in bits. The auld priest roars out, "Murder!" Jock tak's doun the stair as hard as he could bicker, and hides himsel' amang the bees' skeps.

That night, as luck wad have it, some thieves cam' to steal the bees' skeps, and in the hurry o' tumbling them into a large grey plaid, they tumbled Jock in alang wi' them. So aff they set, wi' Jock and the skeps on their backs. On the way, they had to cross the burn where Jock lost his bonnet. Ane o' the thieves cries, "Oh, I hae fand a bonnet!" and Jock, on hearing that, cries out, "Oh, that's mine!" They thocht they had got the deil on their backs. So they let a' fa' in the burn; and Jock, being tied in the plaid, couldna get out; so he and the bees were a' drowned thegither.

If a' tales be true, that's nae lee.

SAINT COLUMBA.

Soon after Saint Columba established his residence in Iona, tradition says that he paid a visit to a great seminary of Druids, then in the vicinity, at a place called Camusnan Ceul, or Bay of Cells, in the district of Ardnamurchan. Several remains of Druidical circles are still to be seen there, and on that bay and the neighbourhood many places are still named after their rites and ceremonies; such as *Ardintibert*, the Mount of Sacrifice, and others. The fame of the Saint had been for some time well known to the people, and his intention of instructing them in the doctrines of Christianity was announced to them. The ancient priesthood made every exertion to dissuade the inhabitants from hearing the powerful eloquence of Columba, and in this they were seconded by the principal man then in that country, whose name was Donald, a son of Connal.

The Saint had no sooner made his appearance, however, than he was surrounded by a vast multitude, anxious to hear so celebrated a preacher; and after the sermon was ended, many persons expressed a desire to be baptized, in spite of the remonstrances of the Druids. Columba had made choice of an eminence centrally situated for performing worship; but there was no water near the spot, and the son of Connal threatened with punishment any who should dare to procure it for his purpose. The Saint stood with his back leaning on a rock; after a short prayer, he struck the rock with his foot, and a stream of water issued forth in great abundance. The miracle had a powerful effect on the minds of his hearers, and many became converts to the new religion. This fountain is still distinguished by the name of Columba, and is considered of superior efficacy in the cure of diseases. When the Catholic form of worship prevailed in that country it was greatly resorted to, and old persons yet remember to have seen offerings left at the fountain in gratitude for benefits received from the benignant influence of the Saint's blessing on the water. At length it is said that a daughter of Donald, the son of Connal, expressed a wish to be baptized, and the father restrained her by violence. He also, with the aid of the Druids, forced Columba to take refuge in his boat, and the holy man departed for Iona, after warning the inhospitable Caledonian to prepare for another world, as his life would soon terminate.

The Saint was at sea during the whole night, which was stormy; and when approaching the shores of his own sacred island the following

Scotch.   F

morning, a vast number of ravens were observed flying over the boat, chasing another of extraordinary large size. The croaking of the ravens awoke the Saint, who had been sleeping; and he instantly exclaimed that the son of Connal had just expired, which was afterwards ascertained to be true.

A very large Christian establishment appears to have been afterwards formed in the Bay of Cells; and the remains of a chapel, dedicated to Saint Kiaran, are still to be seen there. It is the favourite place of interment among the Catholics of this day. Indeed, Columba and many of his successors seem to have adopted the policy of engrafting their institutions on those which had formerly existed in the country. Of this there are innumerable instances, at least we observe the ruins of both still visible in many places; even in Iona we find the burying-ground of the Druids known at the present day. This practice may have had advantages at the time, but it must have been ultimately productive of many corruptions; and, in a great measure, accounts for many superstitious and absurd customs which prevailed among that people to a very recent period, and which are not yet entirely extinct. In a very ancient family in that country two round balls of coarse glass have been carefully preserved from time immemorial, and to these have been ascribed many virtues—amongst others, the cure of any extraordinary disease among cattle. The balls were immersed in cold water for three days and nights, and the water was afterwards sprinkled over all the cattle; this was expected to cure those affected, and to prevent the disease in the rest. From the names and appearance of these balls, there is no doubt that they had been symbols used by the Archdruids.

Within a short distance of the Bay of Cells there is a cave very remarkable in its appearance, and still more so from the purposes to which it has been appropriated. Saint Columba, on one of his many voyages among the Hebrides, was benighted on this rocky coast, and the mariners were alarmed for their own safety. The Saint assured them that neither he nor his crew would ever be drowned. They unexpectedly discovered a light at no great distance, and to that they directed their course. Columba's boat consisted of a frame of osiers, which was covered with hides of leather, and it was received into a very narrow creek close to this cave. After returning thanks for their escape, the Saint and his people had great difficulty in climbing up to the cave, which is elevated considerably above sea. They at length got sight of the fire which had first attracted their attention. Several persons sat around it, and their appearance was not much calculated to please the holy man. Their aspects were fierce, and they had on the fire some flesh roasting over the coals. The Saint gave them his benediction; and he was invited to sit down among them and to share their hurried repast, with which he gladly complied. They were freebooters, who lived by plunder and robbery, and this Columba soon discovered. He advised them to forsake that course, and to be converted to his doctrines, to which they all assented, and in the morning they accompanied the Saint on his voyage homeward. This circumstance created a high veneration for the cave among the disciples and successors of Columba, and that veneration still continues, in some degree. In one side of it there was a cleft of the rock, where lay the water with which the freebooters had been baptized; and this was afterwards formed by art into a basin, which is supplied with water by drops from the roof of the cave. It is alleged never to be empty or to overflow, and the most salubrious qualities are ascribed to it. To obtain the benefit of it, however, the votaries must undergo a very severe ordeal. They must be in the cave before daylight; they stand on the spot where the Saint first landed his boat, and nine waves must dash over their heads; they must afterwards pass through nine openings in the walls of the cave; and, lastly, they must swallow nine mouthfuls out of the holy basin. After invoking the aid of the Saint, the votaries within three weeks are either relieved by death or by recovery. Offerings are left in a certain place appropriated for that purpose; and these are sometimes of considerable value, nor are they ever abstracted. Strangers are always informed that a young man, who had wantonly taken away some of these not many years since, broke his leg before he got home, and this affords the property of the Saint ample protection.

THE MERMAID WIFE.

A STORY is told of an inhabitant of Unst, who, in walking on the sandy margin of a voe, saw a number of mermen and mermaids dancing by moonlight, and several seal-skins strewed beside them on the ground. At his approach they immediately fled to secure their garbs, and, taking upon themselves the form of seals, plunged immediately into the sea. But as the Shetlander perceived that one skin lay close to his feet, he snatched it up, bore it swiftly away, and placed it in concealment. On returning to the shore he met the fairest damsel that was ever gazed upon by mortal eyes, lamenting the robbery, by which she had become an exile from her submarine friends, and a tenant of the upper world. Vainly she implored the restitution of her property; the man had drunk deeply of love, and was inexorable; but he offered her protection beneath his roof as his betrothed spouse. The mer-lady, perceiving that she must become an inhabitant of the earth, found that she could not do better than accept of the offer. This strange attachment subsisted for many years, and the couple had several children. The Shetlander's love for his merwife was unbounded, but his affection was coldly returned. The lady would often steal alone to the desert strand, and, on a signal being given, a large seal would make his appearance, with whom she would hold, in an unknown tongue, an anxious conference. Years had thus glided away, when it happened that one of the children, in the course of his play, found concealed beneath a stack of corn a seal's skin; and, delighted with the prize, he ran with it to his mother. Her eyes glistened with rapture—she gazed upon it as her own—as the means by which she could pass through the ocean that led to her native home. She burst forth into an ecstasy of joy, which was only moderated when she beheld her children, whom she was now about to leave; and, after hastily embracing them, she fled with all speed towards the seaside. The husband immediately returned, learned the discovery that had taken place, ran to overtake his wife, but only arrived in time to see her transformation of shape completed—to see her, in the form of a seal, bound from the ledge of a rock into the sea. The large animal of the same kind with whom she had held a secret converse soon appeared, and evidently congratulated her, in the most tender manner, on her escape. But before she dived to unknown depths, she cast a parting glance at the wretched Shetlander, whose despairing looks excited in her breast a few transient feelings of commiseration.

"Farewell!" said she to him, "and may all good attend you. I loved you very well when I resided upon earth, but I always loved my first husband much better."

THE FIDDLER AND THE BOGLE OF BOGANDORAN.

"Late one night, as my grand-uncle, Lachlan Dhu Macpherson, who was well known as the best fiddler of his day, was returning home from a ball, at which he had acted as a musician, he had occasion to pass through the once-haunted Bog of Torrans. Now, it happened at that time that the bog was frequented by a huge bogle or ghost, who was of a most mischievous disposition, and took particular pleasure in abusing every traveller who had occasion to pass through the place betwixt the twilight at night and cock-crowing in the morning. Suspecting much that he would also come in for a share of his abuse, my grand-uncle made up his mind, in the course of his progress, to return the ghost any *civilities* which he might think meet to offer him. On arriving on the spot, he found his suspicions were too well grounded; for whom did he see but the ghost of Bogandoran apparently ready waiting him, and seeming by his ghastly grin not a little overjoyed at the meeting. Marching up to my grand-uncle, the bogle clapped a huge club into his hand, and furnishing himself with one of the same dimensions, he put a spittle in his hand, and deliberately commenced the combat. My grand-uncle returned the salute with equal spirit, and so ably did both parties ply their batons that for a while the issue of the combat was extremely doubtful. At length, however, the fiddler could easily discover that his opponent's vigour was much in the fagging order. Picking up renewed courage in consequence, he plied the ghost with renewed force, and after a stout resistance, in the course of which both parties were seriously handled, the ghost of Bogandoran thought it prudent to give up the night.

"At the same time, filled no doubt with great indignation at this signal defeat, it seems the ghost resolved to re-engage my grand-uncle on some other occasion, under more favourable circumstances. Not long after, as my grand-uncle was returning home quite unattended from another ball in the Braes of the country, he had just entered the hollow of Auldichoish, well known for its 'eerie' properties, when, lo! who presented himself to his view on the adjacent eminence but his old friend of Bogandoran, advancing as large as the gable of a house, and putting himself in the most threatening and fighting attitudes.

"Looking at the very dangerous nature of the ground where they had met, and feeling no anxiety

for a second encounter with a combatant of his
weight, in a situation so little desirable, the fiddler
would have willingly deferred the settlement of
their differences till a more convenient season.   He,
accordingly, assuming the most submissive aspect in
the world, endeavoured to pass by his champion in
peace, but in vain.   Longing, no doubt, to retrieve
the disgrace of his late discomfiture, the bogle instantly seized the fiddler, and attempted with all
his might to pull the latter down the precipice,
with the diabolical intention, it is supposed, of
drowning him in the river Avon below.   In this
pious design the bogle was happily frustrated by the
intervention of some trees which grew on the precipice, and to which my unhappy grand-uncle clung
with the zeal of a drowning man.   The enraged
ghost, finding it impossible to extricate him from
those friendly trees, and resolving, at all events, to
be revenged upon him, fell upon maltreating the
fiddler with his hands and feet in the most inhuman
manner.

"Such gross indignities my worthy grand-uncle
was not accustomed to, and being incensed beyond
all measure at the liberties taken by Bogandoran,
he resolved again to try his mettle, whether life or
death should be the consequence.   Having no other
weapon wherewith to defend himself but his *biodag*,
which, considering the nature of his opponent's
constitution, he suspected much would be of little

avail to him—I say, in the absence of any other weapon, he sheathed the *biodag* three times in the ghost of Bogandoran's body. And what was the consequence? Why, to the great astonishment of my courageous forefather, the ghost fell down cold dead at his feet, and was never more seen or heard of."

THOMAS THE RHYMER.

THOMAS, of Ercildoun, in Lauderdale, called the Rhymer, on account of his producing a poetical romance on the subject of Tristrem and Yseult, which is curious as the earliest specimen of English verse known to exist, flourished in the reign of Alexander III. of Scotland. Like other men of talent of the period, Thomas was suspected of magic. He was also said to have the gift of prophecy, which was accounted for in the following peculiar manner, referring entirely to the Elfin superstition.

As Thomas lay on Huntly Bank (a place on the descent of the Eildon Hills, which raise their triple crest above the celebrated monastery of Melrose), he saw a lady so extremely beautiful that he imagined she must be the Virgin Mary herself. Her appointments, however, were those rather of an amazon, or goddess of the woods. Her steed was of the highest beauty, and at its mane hung thirty silver bells and nine, which were music to the wind as she paced along. Her saddle was of "royal bone" (ivory), laid over with "orfeverie" (goldsmith's work). Her stirrups, her dress, all corresponded with her extreme beauty and the magnificence of her array. The fair huntress had her bow in hand, and her arrows at her belt. She led three greyhounds in a leash, and three raches, or hounds of scent, followed her closely.

She rejected and disclaimed the homage which Thomas desired to pay her; so that, passing from one extremity to the other, Thomas became as bold as he had at first been humble. The lady warned him he must become her slave if he wished to prosecute his suit. Before their interview terminated, the appearance of the beautiful lady was changed into that of the most hideous hag in existence. A witch from the spital or almshouse would have been a goddess in comparison to the late beautiful huntress. Hideous as she was, Thomas felt that he had placed himself in the power of this hag, and when she bade him take leave of the sun, and of the leaf that grew on the tree, he felt himself under the necessity of obeying her. A cavern received them, in which, following his frightful guide, he for three days travelled in darkness, sometimes hearing the booming of a distant ocean, sometimes walking through rivers of blood, which crossed their subterranean path. At length they emerged into daylight, in a most beautiful orchard. Thomas, almost fainting for want of food, stretched out his hand towards the goodly fruit which hung around him, but was forbidden by his conductress, who informed him that these were the fatal apples which were the cause of the fall of man. He perceived also that his guide had no sooner entered this mysterious ground and breathed its magic air than she was revived in beauty, equipage, and splendour, as fair or fairer than he had first seen her on the mountain. She then proceeded to explain to him the character of the country.

"Yonder right-hand path," she says, "conveys the spirits of the blest to paradise. Yon downward and well-worn way leads sinful souls to the place of everlasting punishment. The third road, by yonder dark brake, conducts to the milder place of pain, from which prayer and mass may release offenders. But see you yet a fourth road, sweeping along the plain to yonder splendid castle? Yonder is the road to Elfland, to which we are now bound. The lord of the castle is king of the country, and I am his queen; and when we enter yonder castle, you must observe strict silence, and answer no question that is asked you, and I will account for your silence by saying I took your speech when I brought you from middle earth."

Having thus instructed him, they journeyed on to the castle, and, entering by the kitchen, found themselves in the midst of such a festive scene as might become the mansion of a great feudal lord or prince.

Thirty carcasses of deer were lying on the massive kitchen board, under the hands of numerous cooks, who toiled to cut them up and dress them, while the gigantic greyhounds which had taken the spoil lay lapping the blood, and enjoying the sight of the slain game. They came next to the royal hall, where the king received his loving consort; knights and ladies, dancing by threes, occupied the floor of the hall; and Thomas, the fatigue of his journey from the Eildon Hills forgotten, went forward and joined in the revelry. After a period, however, which seemed to him a very short one, the queen spoke with him apart, and bade him prepare to return to his own country.

"Now," said the queen, "how long think you that you have been here?"

"Certes, fair lady," answered Thomas, "not above these seven days."

"You are deceived," answered the queen; "you have been seven years in this castle, and it is full time you were gone. Know, Thomas, that the archfiend will come to this castle to-morrow to demand his tribute, and so handsome a man as you will attract his eye. For all the world would I not suffer you to be betrayed to such a fate; therefore up, and let us be going."

This terrible news reconciled Thomas to his departure from Elfinland; and the queen was not long in placing him upon Huntly Bank, where the birds were singing. She took leave of him, and to ensure his reputation bestowed on him the tongue which *could not lie.* Thomas in vain objected to this inconvenient and involuntary adhesion to veracity, which would make him, as he thought, unfit for church or for market, for king's court or for lady's bower. But all his remonstrances were disregarded by the lady; and Thomas the Rhymer, whenever the discourse turned on the future, gained the credit of a prophet whether he would or not, for he could say nothing but what was sure to come to pass.

Thomas remained several years in his own tower near Ercildoun, and enjoyed the fame of his predictions, several of which are current among the country people to this day. At length, as the prophet was entertaining the Earl of March in his dwelling, a cry of astonishment arose in the village, on the appearance of a hart and hind, which left the forest, and, contrary to their shy nature, came quietly onward, traversing the village towards the dwelling of Thomas. The prophet instantly rose from the board, and acknowledging the prodigy as the summons of his fate, he accompanied the hart and hind into the forest, and though occasionally seen by individuals to whom he has chosen to snow himself, he has never again mixed familiarly with mankind.

Scotch.

FAIRY FRIENDS.

IT is a good thing to befriend the fairies, as the following stories show :—

There have been from time immemorial at Hawick, during the two or three last weeks of the year, markets once a week, for the disposal of sheep for slaughter, at which the greater number of people, both in the middle and poorer classes of life, have been accustomed to provide themselves with their *marts*. A poor man from Jedburgh who was on his way to Hawick for the purpose of attending one of these markets, as he was passing over that side of Rubislaw which is nearest the Teviot, was suddenly alarmed by a frightful and unaccountable noise. The sound, as he supposed, proceeded from an immense number of female voices, but no objects whence it could come were visible. Amidst howling and wailing were mixed shouts of mirth and jollity, but he could gather nothing articulate except the following words—

"O there's a bairn born, but there's naething to pit on 't."

The occasion of this elfish concert, it seemed, was the birth of a fairy child, at which the fairies, with the exception of two or three who were discomposed at having nothing to cover the little innocent with, were enjoying themselves with that joviality usually characteristic of such an event. The astonished rustic finding himself amongst a host of invisible beings, in a wild moorland place, and far from any human assistance, should assistance be required, full of the greatest consternation, immediately on hearing this expression again and again vociferated, stripped off his plaid, and threw it on the ground. It was instantly snatched up by an invisible hand, and the wailings immediately ceased, but the shouts of mirth were continued with increased vigour. Being of opinion that what he had done had satisfied his invisible friends, he lost no time in making off, and proceeded on his road to Hawick, musing on his singular adventure. He purchased a sheep, which turned out a remarkably good bargain, and returned to Jedburgh. He had no cause to regret his generosity in bestowing his plaid on the fairies, for every day afterwards his wealth multiplied, and he continued till the day of his death a rich and prosperous man.

About the beginning of harvest, there having been a want of meal for *shearers'* bread in the farmhouse of Bedrule, a small quantity of barley (being all that was yet ripe) was cut down, and converted into meal.   Mrs. Buckham, the farmer's wife, rose early in the morning to bake the bread, and, while she was engaged in baking, a little woman in green costume came in, and, with much politeness, asked for a loan of a capful of meal.   Mrs. Buckham thought it prudent to ·comply with her request.   In a short time afterwards the woman in green returned with an equal quantity of meal, which Mrs. Buckham put into the *meal-ark*.   This meal had such a lasting quality, that from it alone the gudewife of Bedrule baked as much bread as served her own family and the reapers throughout the harvest, and when harvest was over it was not exhausted.

THE SEAL-CATCHER'S ADVENTURE.

THERE was once upon a time a man who lived upon the northern coasts, not far from "Taigh Jan Crot Callow" (John-o'-Groat's House), and he gained his livelihood by catching and killing fish, of all sizes and denominations. He had a particular liking for the killing of those wonderful beasts, half dog half fish, called "Roane," or seals, no doubt because he got a long price for their skins, which are not less curious than they are valuable. The truth is, that the most of these animals are neither dogs nor cods, but downright fairies, as this narration will show; and, indeed, it is easy for any man to convince himself of the fact by a simple examination of his *tobacco-spluichdan*, for the dead skins of those beings are never the same for four-and-twenty hours together. Sometimes the *spluichdan* will erect its bristles almost perpendicularly, while, at other times, it reclines them even down; one time it resembles a bristly sow, at another time a *sleekit cat*; and what dead skin, except itself, could perform such cantrips? Now, it happened one day, as this

notable fisher had returned from the prosecution of
his calling, that he was called upon by a man who
seemed a great stranger, and who said he had been
despatched for him by a person who wished to contract for a quantity of seal-skins, and that the fisher
must accompany him (the stranger) immediately to
see the person who wished to contract for the skins,
as it was necessary that he should be served that
evening. Happy in the prospect of making a good
bargain, and never suspecting any duplicity, he
instantly complied. They both mounted a steed
belonging to the stranger, and took the road with
such velocity that, although the direction of the
wind was towards their backs, yet the fleetness of
their movement made it appear as if it had been in
their faces. On reaching a stupendous precipice
which overhung the sea, his guide told him they
had now reached their destination. .

"Where is the person you spoke of?" inquired
the astonished seal-killer.

"You shall see that presently," replied the guide.

With that they immediately alighted, and, without allowing the seal-killer much time to indulge
the frightful suspicions that began to pervade his
mind, the stranger seized him with irresistible force,
and plunged headlong with him into the sea. After
sinking down, down, nobody knows how far, they
at length reached a door, which, being open, led
them into a range of apartments, filled with inhabi-

tants—not people, but seals, who could nevertheless speak and feel like human folk ; and how much was the seal-killer surprised to find that he himself had been unconsciously transformed into the like image. If it were not so, he would probably have died from the want of breath. The nature of the poor fisher's thoughts may be more easily conceived than described. Looking at the nature of the quarters into which he had landed, all hopes of escape from them appeared wholly chimerical, whilst the degree of comfort, and length of life which the barren scene promised him were far from being flattering. The "Roane," who all seemed in very low spirits, appeared to feel for him, and endeavoured to soothe the distress which he evinced by the amplest assurances of personal safety. Involved in sad meditation on his evil fate, he was quickly roused from his stupor by his guide's producing a huge gully or joctaleg, the object of which he supposed was to put an end to all his earthly cares. Forlorn as was his situation, however, he did not wish to be killed ; and, apprehending instant destruction, he fell down, and earnestly implored for mercy. The poor generous animals did not mean him any harm, however much his former conduct deserved it, and he was accordingly desired to pacify himself, and cease his cries.

"Did you ever see that knife before ?" said the stranger to the fisher.

The latter instantly recognised his own knife, which he had that day stuck into a seal, and with which it had escaped, and acknowledged it was formerly his own, for what would be the use of denying it ?

" Well," rejoined the guide, " the apparent seal which made away with it is my father, who has lain dangerously ill ever since, and no means can stay his fleeting breath without your aid. I have been obliged to resort to the artifice I have practised to bring you hither, and I trust that my filial duty to my father will readily excuse me."

Having said this, he led into another apartment the trembling seal-killer, who expected every minute to be punished for his own ill-treatment of the father. There he found the identical seal with which he had had the encounter in the morning, suffering most grievously from a tremendous cut in its hind-quarter. The seal-killer was then desired, with his hand, to cicatrise the wound, upon doing which it immediately healed, and the seal arose from its bed in perfect health. Upon this the scene changed from mourning to rejoicing—all was mirth and glee. Very different, however, were the feelings of the unfortunate seal-catcher, who expected no doubt to be metamorphosed into a seal for the remainder of his life. However, his late guide accosting him, said—

" Now, sir, you are at liberty to return to your

wife and family, to whom I am about to conduct you ; but it is on this express condition, to which you must bind yourself by a solemn oath, viz. that you will never maim or kill a seal in all your lifetime hereafter."

To this condition, hard as it was, he joyfully acceded ; and the oath being administered in all due form, he bade his new acquaintance most heartily and sincerely a long farewell. Taking hold of his guide, they issued from the place and swam up, till they regained the surface of the sea, and, landing at the said stupendous pinnacle, they found their former steed ready for a second canter. The guide breathed upon the fisher, and they became like men. They mounted their horse, and fleet as had been their course towards the precipice, their return from it was doubly swift ; and the honest seal-killer was laid down at his own door-cheek, where his guide made him such a present as would have almost reconciled him to another similar expedition, such as rendered his loss of profession, in so far as regarded the seals, a far less intolerable hardship than he had at first considered it.

THE FAIRIES OF MERLIN'S CRAIG.

EARLY in the seventeenth century, John Smith, a barn-man at a farm, was sent by his master to cast divots (turf) on the green immediately behind Merlin's Craig. After having laboured for a considerable time, there came round from the front of the rock a little woman, about eighteen inches in height, clad in a green gown and red stockings, with long yellow hair hanging down to her waist, who asked the astonished operator how he would feel were she to send her husband to *tir* (uncover) his house, at the same time commanding him to place every *divot* he had cast *in statu quo*. John obeyed with fear and trembling, and, returning to his master, told what had happened. The farmer laughed at his credulity, and, anxious to cure him of such idle superstition, ordered him to take a cart and fetch home the *divots* immediately.

John obeyed, although with much reluctance. Nothing happened to him in consequence till that day twelve months, when he left his master's work at the usual hour in the evening, with a small *stoup* of milk in his hand, but he did not reach home, nor was he ever heard of for years (I have forgotten how many), when, upon the anniversary of that unfortunate day, John walked into his house at the usual hour, with the milk-stoup in his hand.

The account that he gave of his captivity was that, on the evening of that eventful day, returning home from his labour, when passing Merlin's Craig, he felt himself suddenly taken ill, and sat down to rest a little. Soon after he fell asleep, and awoke, as he supposed, about midnight, when there was a troop of male and female fairies dancing round him. They insisted upon his joining in the sport, and gave him the finest girl in the company as a partner. She took him by the hand; they danced three times round in a fairy ring, after which he became so happy that he felt no inclination to leave his new associates. Their amusements were protracted till he heard his master's cock crow, when the whole troop immediately rushed forward to the front of the craig, hurrying him along with them. A door opened to receive them, and he continued a prisoner until the evening on which he returned, when the same woman who had first appeared to him when casting *divots* came and told him that the grass was again green on the roof of her house, which he had *tirred*, and if he would swear an oath, which she dictated, never to discover what he had seen in fairyland, he should be at liberty to return to his family.

John took the oath, and observed it most religiously, although sadly teased and questioned by his help-mate, particularly about the "bonnie lassie" with whom he danced on the night of his departure. He was also observed to walk a mile out of his way rather than pass Merlin's Craig when the sun was below the horizon.

On a subsequent occasion the tiny inhabitants of Merlin's Craig surprised a shepherd when watching his fold at night; he was asleep, and his bonnet had fallen off and rolled to some little distance. He was awakened by the fairies dancing round him in a circle, and was induced to join them; but re-collecting the fate of John Smith, he would not allow his female companion to take hold of his hands. In the midst of their gambols they came close to the hillock where the shepherd's bonnet lay,—he affected to stumble, fell upon his bonnet, which he immediately seized, clapping it on his head, when the whole troop instantly vanished. This exorcism was produced by the talismanic power of a Catechism containing the Lord's Prayer and the Apostles' Creed, which the shepherd most for-tunately recollected was deposited in the crown of his bonnet.

RORY MACGILLIVRAY.

ONCE upon a time a tenant in the neighbourhood of Cairngorm, in Strathspey, emigrated with his family and cattle to the forest of Glenavon, which is well known to be inhabited by many fairies as well as ghosts. Two of his sons being out late one night in search of some of their sheep which had strayed, had occasion to pass a fairy turret, or dwelling, of very large dimensions; and what was their astonishment on observing streams of the most refulgent light shining forth through innumerable crevices in the rock—crevices which the sharpest eye in the country had never seen before. Curiosity led them towards the turret, when they were charmed by the most exquisite sounds ever emitted by a fiddle-string, which, joined to the sportive mirth and glee accompanying it, reconciled them in a great measure to the scene, although they knew well enough the inhabitants of the nook were fairies. Nay, over-powered by the enchanting jigs played by the fiddler, one of the brothers had even the hardihood to propose that they should pay the occupants of the turret a short visit. To this motion the other brother, fond as he was of dancing, and animated as he was by the music, would by no means consent, and he earnestly desired his brother to restrain his curiosity. But every new jig that was played, and every new reel that was danced, inspired the adventurous brother with additional ardour, and at length, completely fascinated by the enchanting revelry, leaving all prudence behind, at one leap he entered the "Shian." The poor forlorn brother was now left in a most uncomfortable situation. His grief for the loss of a brother whom he dearly loved suggested to him more than once the desperate idea of sharing his fate by following his example. But, on the other hand, when he coolly considered the possibility of sharing very different entertainment from that which rang upon his ears, and remembered, too, the comforts and convenience of his father's fireside, the idea immediately appeared to him anything but prudent. After a long and disagreeable altercation between his affection for his brother and his regard for himself, he came to the resolution to take a middle course, that is, to shout in at the window a few remonstrances to his brother, which, if he did not attend to, let the consequences be upon his own head. Accordingly, taking his station at one of the crevices, and calling upon his brother three several times by name, as use is, he uttered the most moving pieces of elocution he could think of, imploring him, as he valued his poor parents' life and blessing, to come forth and go home with him, Donald Macgillivray, his thrice affectionate and unhappy brother. But whether it was the dancer could not hear this eloquent harangue, or, what is more probable, that he did not choose to attend to it, certain it is that it proved totally ineffectual to accomplish its object, and the consequence was that Donald Macgillivray found it equally his duty and his interest to return home to his family with the melancholy tale of poor Rory's fate. All the prescribed ceremonies calculated to rescue him from the fairy dominion were resorted to by his mourning relatives without effect, and Rory was supposed lost for ever, when a "wise man" of the day having learned the circumstance, discovered to his friends a plan by which they might deliver him at the end of twelve months from his entry.

"Return," says the *Duin Glichd* to Donald, "to the place where you lost your brother a year and a day from the time. You will insert in your garment a *Rowan Cross*, which will protect you from the fairies' interposition. Enter the turret boldly and resolutely in the name of the Highest, claim your brother, and, if he does not accompany you voluntarily, seize him and carry him off by force— none dare interfere with you."

The experiment appeared to the cautious con-

templative brother as one that was fraught with no
ordinary danger, and he would have most willingly
declined the prominent character allotted to him in
the performance but for the importunate entreaty
of his friends, who implored him, as he valued their
blessing, not to slight such excellent advice. Their
entreaties, together with his confidence in the
virtues of the *Rowan Cross*, overcame his scruples,
and he at length agreed to put the experiment in
practice, whatever the result might be.

Well, then, the important day arrived, when the
father of the two sons was destined either to recover
his lost son, or to lose the only son he had, and,
anxious as the father felt, Donald Macgillivray, the
intended adventurer, felt no less so on the occasion.
The hour of midnight approached when the drama
was to be acted, and Donald Macgillivray, loaded
with all the charms and benedictions in his country,
took mournful leave of his friends, and proceeded to
the scene of his intended enterprise. On approaching the well-known turret, a repetition of that mirth
and those ravishing sounds, that had been the
source of so much sorrow to himself and family,
once more attracted his attention, without at all
creating in his mind any extraordinary feelings of
satisfaction. On the contrary, he abhorred the
sounds most heartily, and felt much greater inclination to recede than to advance. But what was to
be done? Courage, character, and everything dear

to him were at stake, so that to advance was his
only alternative. In short, he reached the " Shian,"
and, after twenty fruitless attempts, he at length
entered the place with trembling footsteps, and
amidst the brilliant and jovial scene the not least
gratifying spectacle which presented itself to Donald
was his brother Rory earnestly engaged at the
Highland fling on the floor, at which, as might
have been expected, he had greatly improved.
Without losing much time in satisfying his curiosity
by examining the quality of the company, Donald
ran to his brother, repeating, most vehemently, the
words prescribed to him by the " wise man," seized
him by the collar, and insisted on his immediately
accompanying him home to his poor afflicted parents.
Rory assented, provided he would allow him to
finish his single reel, assuring Donald, very
earnestly, that he had not been half an hour in the
house. In vain did the latter assure him that,
instead of half an hour, he had actually remained
twelve months. Nor would he have believed his
overjoyed friends when his brother at length got
him home, did not the calves, now grown into stots,
and the new-born babes, now travelling the house,
at length convince him that in his single reel he
had danced for a twelvemonth and a day.

Scotch.

H

THE HAUNTED SHIPS.

" Though my mind 's not
Hoodwinked with rustic marvels, I do think
There are more things in the grove, the air, the flood,
Yea, and the charnelled earth, than what wise man,
Who walks so proud as if his form alone
Filled the wide temple of the universe,
Will let a frail mind say. I 'd write i' the creed
O' the sagest head alive, that fearful forms,
Holy or reprobate, do page men's heels ;
That shapes, too horrid for our gaze, stand o'er
The murderer's dust, and for revenge glare up,
Even till the stars weep fire for very pity."

ALONG the sea of Solway, romantic on the Scottish
side, with its woodland, its bays, its cliffs, and head-
lands ; and interesting on the English side, with its
many beautiful towns with their shadows on the
water, rich pastures, safe harbours, and numerous
ships, there still linger many traditional stories of
a maritime nature, most of them connected with
superstitions singularly wild and unusual. To the
curious these tales afford a rich fund of entertainment, from the many diversities of the same story ;
some dry and barren, and stripped of all the embel-
lishments of poetry ; others dressed out in all the
114

riches of a superstitious belief and haunted imagination. In this they resemble the inland traditions of the peasants; but many of the oral treasures of the Galwegian or the Cumbrian coast have the stamp of the Dane and the Norseman upon them, and claim but a remote or faint affinity with the legitimate legends of Caledonia. Something like a rude prosaic outline of several of the most noted of the northern ballads, the adventures and depredations of the old ocean kings, still lends life to the evening tale; and, among others, the story of the Haunted Ships is still popular among the maritime peasantry.

One fine harvest evening I went on board the shallop of Richard Faulder, of Allanbay, and, committing ourselves to the waters, we allowed a gentle wind from the east to waft us at its pleasure towards the Scottish coast. We passed the sharp promontory of Siddick, and, skirting the land within a stonecast, glided along the shore till we came within sight of the ruined Abbey of Sweetheart. The green mountain of Criffel ascended beside us; and the bleat of the flocks from its summit, together with the winding of the evening horn of the reapers, came softened into something like music over land and sea. We pushed our shallop into a deep and wooded bay, and sat silently looking on the serene beauty of the place. The moon glimmered in her rising through the tall shafts of the pines of Caerlaverock; and the sky, with scarce a cloud, showered down on wood and headland and bay the twinkling beams of a thousand stars, rendering every object visible. The tide, too, was coming with that swift and silent swell observable when the wind is gentle; the woody curves along the land were filling with the flood, till it touched the green branches of the drooping trees; while in the centre current the roll and the plunge of a thousand pellocks told to the experienced fisherman that salmon were abundant.

As we looked, we saw an old man emerging from a path that wound to the shore through a grove of doddered hazel; he carried a halve-net on his back, while behind him came a girl, bearing a small harpoon, with which the fishers are remarkably dexterous in striking their prey. The senior seated himself on a large grey stone, which overlooked the bay, laid aside his bonnet, and submitted his bosom and neck to the refreshing sea breeze, and, taking his harpoon from his attendant, sat with the gravity and composure of a spirit of the flood, with his ministering nymph behind him. We pushed our shallop to the shore, and soon stood at their side.

" This is old Mark Macmoran the mariner, with his granddaughter Barbara," said Richard Faulder, in a whisper that had something of fear in it; " he knows every creek and cavern and quicksand in Solway; has seen the Spectre Hound that haunts

the Isle of Man ; has heard him bark, and at every
bark has seen a ship sink ; and he has seen, too, the
Haunted Ships in full sail ; and, if all tales be true,
he has sailed in them himself ;—he 's an awful
person."

Though I perceived in the communication of my
friend something of the superstition of the sailor, I
could not help thinking that common rumour had
made a happy choice in singling out old Mark to
maintain her intercourse with the invisible world.
His hair, which seemed to have refused all intercourse with the comb, hung matted upon his
shoulders ; a kind of mantle, or rather blanket,
pinned with a wooden skewer round his neck, fell
mid-leg down, concealing all his nether garments as
far as a pair of hose, darned with yarn of all con-
ceivable colours, and a pair of shoes, patched and
repaired till nothing of the original structure remained, and clasped on his feet with two massy
silver buckles. If the dress of the old man was rude
and sordid, that of his granddaughter was gay, and
even rich. She wore a bodice of fine wool, wrought
round the bosom with alternate leaf and lily, and a
kirtle of the same fabric, which, almost touching her
white and delicate ankle, showed her snowy feet, so
fairy-light and round that they scarcely seemed to
touch the grass where she stood. Her hair, a natural
ornament which woman seeks much to improve, was
of bright glossy brown, and encumbered rather than

adorned with a snood, set thick with marine productions, among which the small clear pearl found
in the Solway was conspicuous. Nature had not
trusted to a handsome shape and a sylph-like air
for young Barbara's influence over the heart of man,
but had bestowed a pair of large bright blue eyes,
swimming in liquid light, so full of love and gentleness and joy, that all the sailors from Annanwater
to far Saint Bees acknowledged their power, and
sang songs about the bonnie lass of Mark Macmoran.
She stood holding a small gaff-hook of polished
steel in her hand, and seemed not dissatisfied with
the glances I bestowed on her from time to time,
and which I held more than requited by a single
glance of those eyes which retained so many capricious hearts in subjection.

The tide, though rapidly augmenting, had not yet
filled the bay at our feet. The moon now streamed
fairly over the tops of Caerlaverock pines, and
showed the expanse of ocean dimpling and swelling,
on which sloops and shallops came dancing, and
displaying at every turn their extent of white sail
against the beam of the moon. I looked on old
Mark the mariner, who, seated motionless on his
grey stone, kept his eye fixed on the increasing
waters with a look of seriousness and sorrow, in
which I saw little of the calculating spirit of a mere
fisherman. Though he looked on the coming tide,
his eyes seemed to dwell particularly on the black

and decayed hulls of two vessels, which, half immersed in the quicksand, still addressed to every
heart a tale of shipwreck and desolation. The tide
wheeled and foamed around them, and, creeping inch
by inch up the side, at last fairly threw its waters
over the top, and a long and hollow eddy showed
the resistance which the liquid element received.

The moment they were fairly buried in the water,
the old man clasped his hands together, and said :
" Blessed be the tide that will break over and bury
ye for ever! Sad to mariners, and sorrowful to
maids and mothers, has the time been you have
choked up this deep and bonnie bay. For evil were
you sent, and for evil have you continued. Every
season finds from you its song of sorrow and wail,
its funeral processions, and its shrouded corses.
Woe to the land where the wood grew that made
ye! Cursed be the axe that hewed ye on the
mountains, the hands that joined ye together, the
bay that ye first swam in, and the wind that wafted
ye here! Seven times have ye put my life in peril,
three fair sons have ye swept from my side, and two
bonnie grand-bairns ; and now, even now, your
waters foam and flash for my destruction, did I
venture my infirm limbs in quest of food in your
deadly bay. I see by that ripple and that foam,
and hear by the sound and singing of your surge,
that ye yearn for another victim ; but it shall not
be me nor mine."

Even as the old mariner addressed himself to the wrecked ships, a young man appeared at the southern extremity of the bay, holding his halve-net in his hand, and hastening into the current. Mark rose and shouted, and waved him back from a place which, to a person unacquainted with the dangers of the bay, real and superstitious, seemed sufficiently perilous ; his granddaughter, too, added her voice to his, and waved her white hands ; but the more they strove, the faster advanced the peasant, till he stood to his middle in the water, while the tide increased every moment in depth and strength. " Andrew, Andrew," cried the young woman, in a voice quavering with emotion, " turn, turn, I tell you ! O the Ships, the Haunted Ships ! " But the appearance of a fine run of fish had more influence with the peasant than the voice of bonnie Barbara, and forward he dashed, net in hand. In a moment he was borne off his feet, and mingled like foam with the water, and hurried towards the fatal eddies which whirled and roared round the sunken ships. But he was a powerful young man, and an expert swimmer ; he seized on one of the projecting ribs of the nearest hulk, and clinging to it with the grasp of despair, uttered yell after yell, sustaining himself against the prodigious rush of the current.

From a shealing of turf and straw, within the pitch of a bar from the spot where we stood, came out an old woman bent with age, and leaning on a crutch. "I heard the voice of that lad Andrew Lammie; can the chield be drowning that he skirls sae uncannily?" said the old woman, seating herself on the ground, and looking earnestly at the water. "Ou, ay," she continued, "he's doomed, he's doomed; heart and hand can never save him; boats, ropes, and man's strength and wit, all vain! vain! —he's doomed, he's doomed!"

By this time I had thrown myself into the shallop, followed reluctantly by Richard Faulder, over whose courage and kindness of heart superstition had great power, and with one push from the shore, and some exertion in sculling, we came within a quoitcast of the unfortunate fisherman. He stayed not to profit by our aid; for, when he perceived us near, he uttered a piercing shriek of joy, and bounded towards us through the agitated element the full length of an oar. I saw him for a second on the surface of the water, but the eddying current sucked him down; and all I ever beheld of him again was his hand held above the flood, and clutching in agony at some imaginary aid. I sat gazing in horror on the vacant sea before us; but a breathing-time before, a human being, full of youth and strength and hope, was there; his cries were still ringing in my ears, and echoing in the woods; and now nothing was seen or heard save the turbulent expanse of water, and the sound of its chafing on the shores. We pushed back our shallop, and resumed our station on the cliff beside the old mariner and his descendant.

"Wherefore sought ye to peril your own lives fruitlessly," said Mark, "in attempting to save the doomed? Whoso touches those infernal ships never survives to tell the tale. Woe to the man who is found nigh them at midnight when the tide has subsided, and they arise in their former beauty, with forecastle, and deck, and sail, and pennon, and shroud! Then is seen the streaming of lights along the water from their cabin windows, and then is heard the sound of mirth and the clamour of tongues, and the infernal whoop and halloo and song, ringing far and wide. Woe to the man who comes nigh them!"

To all this my Allanbay companion listened with a breathless attention. I felt something touched with a superstition to which I partly believed I had seen one victim offered up; and I inquired of the old mariner, "How and when came these Haunted Ships there? To me they seem but the melancholy relics of some unhappy voyagers, and much more likely to warn people to shun destruction than entice and delude them to it."

"And so," said the old man with a smile, which had more of sorrow in it than of mirth; "and so, young man, these black and shattered hulks seem to the eye of the multitude. But things are not what they seem: that water, a kind and convenient

servant to the wants of man, which seems so smooth
and so dimpling and so gentle, has swallowed up a
human soul even now; and the place which it
covers, so fair and so level, is a faithless quicksand,
out of which none escape. Things are otherwise
than they seem. Had you lived as long as I have
had the sorrow to live; had you seen the storms,
and braved the perils, and endured the distresses
which have befallen me; had you sat gazing out on
the dreary ocean at midnight on a haunted coast;
had you seen comrade after comrade, brother after
brother, and son after son, swept away by the
merciless ocean from your very side; had you seen
the shapes of friends, doomed to the wave and the
quicksand, appearing to you in the dreams and
visions of the night, then would your mind have
been prepared for crediting the maritime legends of
mariners; and the two haunted Danish ships would
have had their terrors for you, as they have for all
who sojourn on this coast.

"Of the time and the cause of their destruction,"
continued the old man, "I know nothing certain;
they have stood as you have seen them for un-
counted time; and while all other ships wrecked
on this unhappy coast have gone to pieces, and
rotted and sunk away in a few years, these two
haunted hulks have neither sunk in the quicksand,
nor has a single spar or board been displaced.
Maritime legend says that two ships of Denmark

having had permission, for a time, to work deeds of
darkness and dolor on the deep, were at last
condemned to the whirlpool and the sunken rock,
and were wrecked in this bonnie bay, as a sign to
seamen to be gentle and devout. The night when
they were lost was a harvest evening of uncommon
mildness and beauty : the sun had newly set; the
moon came brighter and brighter out; and the
reapers, laying their sickles at the root of the standing corn, stood on rock and bank, looking at the
increasing magnitude of the waters, for sea and land
were visible from Saint Bees to Barnhourie. The
sails of two vessels were soon seen bent for the
Scottish coast ; and, with a speed outrunning the
swiftest ship, they approached the dangerous quick-
sands and headland of Borranpoint. On the deck
of the foremost ship not a living soul was seen, or
shape, unless something in darkness and form resembling a human shadow could be called a shape,
which flitted from extremity to extremity of the
ship, with the appearance of trimming the sails, and
directing the vessel's course. But the decks of its
companion were crowded with human shapes ; the
captain and mate, and sailor and cabin-boy, all
seemed there ; and from them the sound of mirth and
minstrelsy echoed over land and water. The coast
which they skirted along was one of extreme danger,
and the reapers shouted to warn them to beware of
sandbank and rock ; but of this friendly counsel no

notice was taken, except that a large and famished dog, which sat on the prow, answered every shout with a long, loud, and melancholy howl. The deep sandbank of Carsethorn was expected to arrest the career of these desperate navigators; but they passed, with the celerity of water-fowl, over an obstruction which had wrecked many pretty ships.

" Old men shook their heads and departed, saying, ' We have seen the fiend sailing in a bottomless ship ; let us go home and pray ; ' but one young and wilful man said, ' Fiend ! I 'll warrant it 's nae fiend, but douce Janet Withershins the witch, hold. ing a carouse with some of her Cumberland cummers, and mickle red wine will be spilt atween them. Dod I would gladly have a toothfu'! I 'll warrant it 's nane o' your cauld sour slae-water like a bottle of Bailie Skrinkie's port, but right drap-o'-my-heart's-blood stuff, that would waken a body out of their last linen. I wonder where the cummers will anchor their craft ? ' ' And I 'll vow,' said another rustic, ' the wine they quaff is none of your visionary drink, such as a drouthie body has dished out to his lips in a dream; nor is it shadowy and unsubstantial, like the vessels they sail in, which are made out of a cockel-shell or a cast-off slipper, or the paring of a seaman's right thumb-nail. I once got a hansel out of a witch's quaigh myself—auld Marion Mathers, of Dustiefoot, whom they tried to bury in the old kirkyard of

Dunscore ; but the cummer raise as fast as they
laid her down, and naewhere else would she lie but
in the bonnie green kirkyard of Kier, among douce
and sponsible fowk. So I'll vow that the wine of a
witch's cup is as fell liquor as ever did a kindly
turn to a poor man's heart ; and be they fiends, or
be they witches, if they have red wine asteer, I'll
risk a drouket sark for ae glorious tout on 't."

" ' Silence, ye sinners,' said the minister's son of a
neighbouring parish, who united in his own person
his father's lack of devotion with his mother's love
of liquor. ' Whist !—speak as if ye had the fear of
something holy before ye. Let the vessels run
their own way to destruction : who can stay the
eastern wind, and the current of the Solway sea ?
I can find ye Scripture warrant for that ; so let
them try their strength on Blawhooly rocks, and
their might on the broad quicksand. There 's a
surf running there would knock the ribs together of
a galley built by the imps of the pit, and commanded
by the Prince of Darkness. Bonnily and bravely
they sail away there, but before the blast blows by
they 'll be wrecked ; and red wine and strong brandy
will be as rife as dyke-water, and we 'll drink the
health of bonnie Bell Blackness out of her left-foot
slipper.'

" The speech of the young profligate was ap-
plauded by several of his companions, and away
they flew to the bay of Blawhooly, from whence they

never returned. The two vessels were observed all at once to stop in the bosom of the bay, on the spot where their hulls now appear; the mirth and the minstrelsy waxed louder than ever, and the forms of maidens, with instruments of music and wine-cups in their hands, thronged the decks. A boat was lowered; and the same shadowy pilot who conducted the ships made it start towards the shore with the rapidity of lightning, and its head knocked against the bank where the four young men stood who longed for the unblest drink. They leaped in with a laugh, and with a laugh were they welcomed on deck; wine-cups were given to each, and as they raised them to their lips the vessels melted away beneath their feet, and one loud shriek, mingled with laughter still louder, was heard over land and water for many miles. Nothing more was heard or seen till the morning, when the crowd who came to the beach saw with fear and wonder the two Haunted Ships, such as they now seem, masts and tackle gone; nor mark, nor sign, by which their name, country, or destination could be known, was left remaining. Such is the tradition of the mariners; and its truth has been attested by many families whose sons and whose fathers have been drowned in the haunted bay of Blawhooly."

"And trow ye," said the old woman, who, atracted from her hut by the drowning cries of the young fisherman, had remained an auditor of the

mariner's legend,—"And trow ye, Mark Macmoran,
that the tale of the Haunted Ships is done? I can
say no to that. Mickle have mine ears heard;
but more mine eyes have witnessed since I came to
dwell in this humble home by the side of the deep
sea. I mind the night weel; it was on Hallowmas
Eve; the nuts were cracked, and the apples were
eaten, and spell and charm were tried at my fireside; till, wearied with diving into the dark waves
of futurity, the lads and lasses fairly took to the
more visible blessings of kind words, tender clasps,
and gentle courtship. Soft words in a maiden's
ear, and a kindly kiss o' her lip were old-world
matters to me, Mark Macmoran; though I mean
not to say that I have been free of the folly of
daunering and daffin with a youth in my day, and
keeping tryst with him in dark and lonely places.
However, as I say, these times of enjoyment were
passed and gone with me—the mair's the pity that
pleasure should fly sae fast away—and as I couldna make sport I thought I should not mar any; so
out I sauntered into the fresh cold air, and sat down
behind that old oak, and looked abroad on the wide
sea. I had my ain sad thoughts, ye may think, at
the time: it was in that very bay my blythe goodman perished, with seven more in his company;
and on that very bank where ye see the waves leaping and foaming, I saw seven stately corses streeked,
but the dearest was the eighth. It was a woful

sight to me, a widow, with four bonnie boys, with nought to support them but these twa hands, and God's blessing, and a cow's grass. I have never liked to live out of sight of this bay since that time ; and mony's the moonlight night I sit looking on these watery mountains and these waste shores; it does my heart good, whatever it may do to my head. So ye see it was Hallowmas Night, and looking on sea and land sat I ; and my heart wandering to other thoughts soon made me forget my youthful company at hame. It might be near the howe hour of the night. The tide was making, and its singing brought strange old-world stories with it, and I thought on the dangers that sailors endure, the fates they meet with, and the fearful forms they see. My own blythe goodman had seen sights that made him grave enough at times, though he aye tried to laugh them away.

"Aweel, atween that very rock aneath us and the coming tide, I saw, or thought I saw—for the tale is so dreamlike that the whole might pass for a vision of the night,—I saw the form of a man ; his plaid was grey, his face was grey ; and his hair, which hung low down till it nearly came to the middle of his back, was as white as the white seafoam. He began to howk and dig under the bank ; an' God be near me, thought I, this maun be the unblessed spirit of auld Adam Gowdgowpin the miser, who is doomed to dig for shipwrecked treasure,

Scotch.

I

and count how many millions are hidden for ever
from man's enjoyment. The form found something
which in shape and hue seemed a left-foot slipper
of brass; so down to the tide he marched, and,
placing it on the water, whirled it thrice round, and
the infernal slipper dilated at every turn, till it
became a bonnie barge with its sails bent, and on
board leaped the form, and scudded swiftly away.
He came to one of the Haunted Ships, and striking
it with his oar, a fair ship, with mast and canvas
and mariners, started up; he touched the other
Haunted Ship, and produced the like transformation; and away the three spectre ships bounded,
leaving a track of fire behind them on the billows
which was long unextinguished. Now wasna
that a bonnie and fearful sight to see beneath the
light of the Hallowmas moon? But the tale is
far frae finished, for mariners say that once a year,
on a certain night, if ye stand on the Borran Point,
ye will see the infernal shallops coming snoring
through the Solway; ye will hear the same laugh and
song and mirth and minstrelsy which our ancestors
heard; see them bound over the sandbanks and
sunken rocks like sea-gulls, cast their anchor in
Blawhooly Bay, while the shadowy figure lowers
down the boat, and augments their numbers with
the four unhappy mortals to whose memory a stone
stands in the kirkyard, with a sinking ship and a
shoreless sea cut upon it. Then the spectre ships

vanish, and the drowning shriek of mortals and the
rejoicing laugh of fiends are heard, and the old hulls
are left as a memorial that the old spiritual kingdom has not departed from the earth. But I maun
away, and trim my little cottage fire, and make it
burn and blaze up bonnie, to warm the crickets and
my cold and crazy bones that maun soon be laid
aneath the green sod in the eerie kirkyard." And
away the old dame tottered to her cottage, secured
the door on the inside, and soon the hearth-flame
was seen to glimmer and gleam through the keyhole
and window.

"I'll tell ye what," said the old mariner, in a
subdued tone, and with a shrewd and suspicious
glance of his eye after the old sibyl, "it's a word
that may not very well be uttered, but there are
many mistakes made in evening stories if old Moll
Moray there, where she lives, knows not mickle
more than she is willing to tell of the Haunted Ships
and their unhallowed mariners. She lives cannily
and quietly; no one knows how she is fed or sup-
ported; but her dress is aye whole, her cottage ever
smokes, and her table lacks neither of wine, white
and red, nor of fowl and fish, and white bread and
brown. It was a dear scoff to Jock Matheson,
when he called old Moll the uncanny carline of
Blawhooly: his boat ran round and round in the
centre of the Solway—everybody said it was enchanted—and down it went head foremost; and

hadna Jock been a swimmer equal to a sheldrake, he would have fed the fish. But I'll warrant it sobered the lad's speech; and he never reckoned himself safe till he made old Moll the present of a new kirtle and a stone of cheese."

"O father!" said his granddaughter Barbara, "ye surely wrong poor old Mary Moray; what use could it be to an old woman like her, who has no wrongs to redress, no malice to work out against mankind, and nothing to seek of enjoyment save a canny hour and a quiet grave—what use could the fellowship of fiends and the communion of evil spirits be to her? I know Jenny Primrose puts rowan-tree above the door-head when she sees old Mary coming; I know the goodwife of Kittlenaket wears rowan-berry leaves in the headband of her blue kirtle, and all for the sake of averting the un- sonsie glance of Mary's right ee; and I know that the auld Laird of Burntroutwater drives his seven cows to their pasture with a wand of witch-tree, to keep Mary from milking them. But what has all that to do with haunted shallops, visionary mariners, and bottomless boats? I have heard myself as pleasant a tale about the Haunted Ships and their unworldly crews as any one would wish to hear in a winter evening. It was told me by young Benjie Macharg, one summer night, sitting on Arbigland- bank: the lad intended a sort of love meeting; but all that he could talk of was about smearing sheep

and shearing sheep, and of the wife which the
Norway elves of the Haunted Ships made for his
uncle Sandie Macharg. And I shall tell ye the tale
as the honest lad told it to me.

"Alexander Macharg, besides being the laird of
three acres of peatmoss, two kale gardens, and the
owner of seven good milch cows, a pair of horses,
and six pet sheep, was the husband of one of the
handsomest women in seven parishes. Many a lad
sighed the day he was brided; and a Nithsdale
laird and two Annandale moorland farmers drank
themselves to their last linen, as well as their last
shilling, through sorrow for her loss. But married
was the dame; and home she was carried, to bear
rule over her home and her husband, as an honest
woman should. Now ye maun ken that though
the flesh-and-blood lovers of Alexander's bonnie
wife all ceased to love and to sue her after she
became another's, there were certain admirers who
did not consider their claim at all abated, or their
hopes lessened by the kirk's famous obstacle of
matrimony. Ye have heard how the devout
minister of Tinwald had a fair son carried away,
and wedded against his liking to an unchristened
bride, whom the elves and the fairies provided; ye
have heard how the bonnie bride of the drunken
Laird of Soukitup was stolen by the fairies out at
the back-window of the bridal chamber, the time
the bridegroom was groping his way to the chamber

door; and ye have heard—but why need I multiply cases? Such things in the ancient days were as common as candle-light. So ye 'll no hinder certain water elves and sea fairies, who sometimes keep festival and summer mirth in these old haunted hulks, from falling in love with the weel-faured wife of Laird Macharg; and to their plots and contrivances they went how they might accomplish to sunder man and wife; and sundering such a man and such a wife was like sundering the green leaf from the summer, or the fragrance from the flower.

"So it fell on a time that Laird Macharg took his halve-net on his back, and his steel spear in his hand, and down to Blawhooly Bay gaed he, and into the water he went right between the two haunted hulks, and placing his net awaited the coming of the tide. The night, ye maun ken, was mirk, and the wind lowne, and the singing of the increasing waters among the shells and the peebles was heard for sundry miles. All at once light began to glance and twinkle on board the two Haunted Ships from every hole and seam, and presently the sound as of a hatchet employed in squaring timber echoed far and wide. But if the toil of these unearthly workmen amazed the laird, how much more was his amazement increased when a sharp shrill voice called out, 'Ho, brother! what are you doing now?' A voice still shriller responded from the other haunted ship, 'I 'm making

a wife to Sandie Macharg!' And a loud quavering
laugh running from ship to ship, and from bank to
bank, told the joy they expected from their labour.

"Now the laird, besides being a devout and a
God-fearing man, was shrewd and bold; and in
plot and contrivance, and skill in conducting his
designs, was fairly an overmatch for any dozen land
elves; but the water elves are far more subtle;
besides their haunts and their dwellings being in
the great deep, pursuit and detection is hopeless if
they succeed in carrying their prey to the waves.
But ye shall hear. Home flew the laird, collected
his family around the hearth, spoke of the signs and
the sins of the times, and talked of mortification
and prayer for averting calamity; and, finally, taking his father's Bible, brass clasps, black print, and
covered with calf-skin, from the shelf, he proceeded
without let or stint to perform domestic worship. I
should have told ye that he bolted and locked the
door, shut up all inlet to the house, threw salt into
the fire, and proceeded in every way like a man
skilful in guarding against the plots of fairies and
fiends. His wife looked on all this with wonder;
but she saw something in her husband's looks that
hindered her from intruding either question or
advice, and a wise woman was she.

"Near the mid-hour of the night the rush of a
horse's feet was heard, and the sound of a rider
leaping from its back, and a heavy knock came to

the door, accompanied by a voice, saying, ' The
cummer drink's hot, and the knave bairn is expected at Laird Laurie's to-night ; sae mount, goodwife, and come.'

" ' Preserve me ! ' said the wife of Sandie Macharg, ' that's news indeed ; who could have thought
it ? The laird has been heirless for seventeen years !
Now, Sandie, my man, fetch me my skirt and hood.'

" But he laid his arm round his wife's neck, and
said, ' If all the lairds in Galloway go heirless, over
this door threshold shall you not stir to-night ; and
I have said, and I have sworn it ; seek not to know
why or wherefore—but, Lord, send us thy blessed
mornlight.' The wife looked for a moment in her
husband's eyes, and desisted from further entreaty.

" ' But let us send a civil message to the gossips,
Sandy ; and hadna ye better say I am sair laid
with a sudden sickness ? though it's sinful-like to
send the poor messenger a mile agate with a lie in
his mouth without a glass of brandy.'

" ' To such a messenger, and to those who sent
him, no apology is needed,' said the austere laird ;
'so let him depart.' And the clatter of a horse's
hoofs was heard, and the muttered imprecations of
its rider on the churlish treatment he had experienced.

" ' Now, Sandie, my lad,' said his wife, laying an
arm particularly white and round about his neck as
she spoke, ' are you not a queer man and a stern ?

I have been your wedded wife now these three
years; and, beside my dower, have brought you
three as bonnie bairns as ever smiled aneath a
summer sun. O man, you a douce man, and fitter
to be an elder than even Willie Greer himself, I
have the minister's ain word for 't, to put on these
hard-hearted looks, and gang waving your arms
that way, as if ye said, "I winna take the counsel
of sic a hempie as you;" I'm your ain leal wife,
and will and maun have an explanation.'

"To all this Sandie Macharg replied, 'It is
written, "Wives, obey your husbands"; but we
have been stayed in our devotion, so let us pray;'
and down he knelt: his wife knelt also, for she was
as devout as bonnie; and beside them knelt their
household, and all lights were extinguished.

"'Now this beats a',' muttered his wife to herself; 'however, I shall be obedient for a time; but
if I dinna ken what all this is for before the morn
by sunket-time, my tongue is nae langer a tongue,
nor my hands worth wearing.'

"The voice of her husband in prayer interrupted
this mental soliloquy; and ardently did he beseech
to be preserved from the wiles of the fiends and the
snares of Satan; from witches, ghosts, goblins,
elves, fairies, spunkies, and water-kelpies; from the
spectre shallop of Solway; from spirits visible and
invisible; from the Haunted Ships and their unearthly tenants; from maritime spirits that plotted

against godly men, and fell in love with their wives——'

"'Nay, but His presence be near us!' said his wife, in a low tone of dismay. 'God guide my gudeman's wits : I never heard such a prayer from human lips before. But, Sandie, my man, Lord's sake, rise. What fearful light is this? Barn and byre and stable maun be in a blaze; and Hawkie, and Hurley, Doddie, and Cherrie, and Damsonplum will be smoored with reek, and scorched with flame.'

"And a flood of light, but not so gross as a common fire, which ascended to heaven and filled all the court before the house, amply justified the goodwife's suspicions. But to the terrors of fire Sandie was as immovable as he was to the imaginary groans of the barren wife of Laird Laurie; and he held his wife, and threatened the weight of his right hand—and it was a heavy one—to all who ventured abroad, or even unbolted the door. The neighing and prancing of horses, and the bellowing of cows, augmented the horrors of the night; and to any one who only heard the din, it seemed that the whole onstead was in a blaze, and horses and cattle perishing in the flame. All wiles, common or extraordinary, were put in practice to entice or force the honest farmer and his wife to open the door; and when the like success attended every new stratagem, silence for a little while ensued, and a long, loud, and shrilling laugh wound up the dramatic efforts of the night. In the morning, when Laird Macharg went to the door, he found standing against one of the pilasters a piece of black ship oak, rudely fashioned into something like human form, and which skilful people declared would have been clothed with seeming flesh and blood, and palmed upon him by elfin adroitness for his wife, had he admitted his visitants. A synod of wise men and women sat upon the woman of timber, and she was finally ordered to be devoured by fire, and that in the open air. A fire was soon made, and into it the elfin sculpture was tossed from the prongs of two pairs of pitchforks. The blaze that arose was awful to behold ; and hissings and burstings and loud cracklings and strange noises were heard in the midst of the flame ; and when the whole sank into ashes, a drinking-cup of some precious metal was found ; and this cup, fashioned no doubt by elfin skill, but rendered harmless by the purification with fire, the sons and daughters of Sandie Macharg and his wife drink out of to this very day. Bless all bold men, say I, and obedient wives !"

THE BROWNIE.

THE Scottish Brownie formed a class of being distinct in habit and disposition from the freakish and mischievous elves. He was meagre, shaggy, and wild in his appearance. Thus Cleland, in his satire against the Highlanders, compares them to

> "Faunes, or Brownies, if ye will,
> Or Satyres come from Atlas Hill."

In the day-time he lurked in remote recesses of the old houses which he delighted to haunt, and in the night sedulously employed himself in discharging any laborious task which he thought might be acceptable to the family to whose service he had devoted himself. But the Brownie does not drudge from the hope of recompense. On the contrary, so delicate is his attachment that the offer of reward, but particularly of food, infallibly occasions his disappearance for ever. It is told of a Brownie, who haunted a border family now extinct, that the lady having fallen unexpectedly ill, and the servant, who was ordered to ride to Jedburgh for the *sage-femme*, showing no great alertness in setting out,

140

the familiar spirit slipped on the greatcoat of the lingering domestic, rode to the town on the laird's best horse, and returned with the midwife *en croupe*. During the short space of his absence, the Tweed, which they must necessarily ford, rose to a dangerous height. Brownie, who transported his charge with all the rapidity of the ghostly lover of Lenore, was not to be stopped by the obstacle. He plunged in with the terrified old lady, and landed her in safety where her services were wanted. Having put the horse into the stable (where it was afterwards found in a woful plight), he proceeded to the room of the servant, whose duty he had discharged, and finding him just in the act of drawing on his boots, he administered to him a most merciless drubbing with his own horsewhip. Such an important service excited the gratitude of the laird, who, understanding that Brownie had been heard to express a wish to have a green coat, ordered a vestment of the colour to be made, and left in his haunts. Brownie took away the green coat, but was never seen more. We may suppose that, tired of his domestic drudgery, he went in his new livery to join the fairies.

The last Brownie known in Ettrick Forest resided in Bodsbeck, a wild and solitary spot, near the head of Moffat Water, where he exercised his functions undisturbed, till the scrupulous devotion of an old lady induced her to "hire him away," as it was termed, by placing in his haunt a porringer of milk and a piece of money. After receiving this hint to depart, he was heard the whole night to howl and cry, "Farewell to bonnie Bodsbeck!" which he was compelled to abandon for ever.

MAUNS' STANE.

In the latter end of the autumn of 18—, I set out by myself on an excursion over the northern part of Scotland, and during that time my chief amusement was to observe the little changes of manners, language, etc., in the different districts. After having viewed on my return the principal curiosities in Buchan, I made a little ale-house, or "public," my head-quarters for the night. Having discussed my supper in solitude, I called up mine host to enable me to discuss my bottle, and to give me a statistical account of the country around me. Seated in the "blue" end, and well supplied with the homely but satisfying luxuries which the place afforded, I was in an excellent mood for enjoying the communicativeness of my landlord; and, after speaking about the cave of Slaines, the state of the crops, and the neighbouring franklins, edged him, by degrees, to speak about the Abbey of Deer, an interesting ruin which I had examined in the course of the day, formerly the stronghold of the once powerful family of Cummin.

143

"It's dootless a bonnie place about the abbey," said he, "but naething like what it was when the great Sir James the Rose came to hide i' the Buchan woods wi' a' the Grahames rampagin' at his tail, whilk you that's a beuk-learned man 'ill hae read o', an' may be ye'll hae heard o' the saughen bush where he forgathered wi' his jo; or aiblins ye may have seen't, for it's standing yet just at the corner o' gaukit Jamie Jamieson's peat-stack. Ay, ay, the abbey was a brave place once; but a' thing, ye ken, comes till an end." So saying, he nodded to me, and brought his glass to an end.

"This place, then, must have been famed in days of yore, my friend?"

"Ye may tak my word for that," said he, "'Od, it *was* a place! Sic a sight o' fechtin' as they had about it! But gin ye'll gan up the trap-stair to the laft, an' open Jenny's kist, ye'll see sic a story about it, printed by ane o' your learned Aberdeen's fouk, Maister Keith, I think; she coft it in Aberdeen for twal' pennies, lang ago, an' battered it to the lid o' her kist. But gang up the stair canny, for fear that you should wauken her, puir thing; or, bide, I'll just wauken Jamie Fleep, an' gar him help me down wi't, for our stair's no just that canny for them 't's no acquaint wi't, let alane a frail man wi' your infirmity."

I assured him that I would neither disturb the young lady's slumber nor Jamie Fleep's, and begged

him to give me as much information as he could
about this castle.

"Weel, wishin' your guid health again.—Our
minister ance said that Solomon's Temple was a' in
ruins, wi' whin bushes, an' broom and thistles growin'
ower the bonnie carved wark an' the cedar wa's, just
like our ain abbey. Noo, I judge that the Abbey o'
Deer was just the marrow o 't, or the minister wadna
hae said that. But when it was biggit, Lord kens,
for I dinna. It was just as you see it, lang afore
your honour was born, an' aiblins, as the by-word
says, may be sae after ye 're hauged. But that's
neither here nor there. The Cummins o' Buchan
were a dour and surly race; and, for a fearfu' time,
nane near han' nor far awa could ding them, an' yet
mony a ane tried it. The fouk on their ain lan'
likit them weel enough; but the Crawfords, an' the
Grahames, an' the Mars, an' the Lovats, were aye
trying to comb them against the hair, an' mony a
weary kempin' had they wi' them. But some way
or ither they could never ding them; an' fouk said
that they gaed and learned the black art frae the
Pope o' Room, wha, I myself heard the minister say,
had aye a colleague wi' the Auld Chiel. I dinna
ken fou it was, in the tail o' the day, the hale country
raise up against them, an' besieged them in the
Abbey o' Deer. Ye 'll see, my frien'" (by this time
mine host considered me as one of his cronies),
"tho' we ca' it the abbey, it had naething to do wi'

Scotch.

K

papistry; na, na, no sae bad as a' that either, but just a noble's castle, where they keepit sodgers gaun about in airn an' scarlet, wi' their swords an' guns, an' begnets, an' sentry-boxes, like the local militia in the barracks o' Aberdeen.

"Weel, ye see, they surrounded the castle, an' lang did they besiege it; but there was a vast o' meat in the castle, an' the Buchan fouk fought like the vera deil. They took their horse through a miscellaneous passage, half a mile long, aneath the hill o' Saplinbrae, an' watered them in the burn o' Pulmer. But a' wadna do; they took the castle at last, and a terrible slaughter they made amo' them; but they were sair disappointed in ae partic'ler, for Cummin's fouk sank a' their goud an' siller in a draw-wall, an' syne filled it up wi' stanes. They got naething in the way of spulzie to speak o'; sae out o' spite they dang doon the castle, an' it's never been biggit to this day. But the Cummins were no sae bad as the Lairds o' Federat, after a'."

"And who were these Federats?" I inquired.

"The Lairds o' Federat?" said he, moistening his mouth again as a preamble to his oration. "Troth, frae their deeds ane would maist think that they had a drap o' the deil's blude, like the pyets. Gin a' tales be true, they hae the warmest place at his bink this vera minute. I dinna ken vera muckle about them though, but the auldest fouk said they were just byous wi' cruelty. Mony a good man did

they hing up i' their ha', just for their ain sport;
ye 'll see the ring to the fore yet in the roof o 't.
Did ye never hear o' Mauns' Stane, neebour?"

" Mauns' what?" said I.

" Ou, Mauns' Stane. But it 's no likely. Ye see
it was just a queer clump o' a roun'-about heathen,
waghlin' may be twa tons or thereby. It wasna like
ony o' the stanes in our countra, an' it was as roun'
as a fit-ba'; I 'm sure it wad ding Professor Couplan
himsel' to tell what way it cam' there. Noo, fouk
aye thought there was something uncanny about it,
an' some gaed the length o' saying that the deil used
to bake ginshbread upon 't; and, as sure as ye 're
sitting there, frien', there was knuckle-marks upon 't,
for my ain father has seen them as aften as I have
taes an' fingers. Aweel, ye see, Mauns Crawford,
the last o' the Lairds o' Federat, an' the deil had
coost out (may be because the laird was just as
wicked an' as clever as he was himsel'), an' ye per-
ceive the evil ane wantit to play him a trick. Noo,
Mauns Crawford was ae day lookin' ower his castle
wa', and he saw a stalwart carle, in black claes, ridin'
up the loanin'. He stopped at this chuckie o' a
stane, an' loutin' himsel', he took it up in his arms,
and lifted it three times to his saddle-bow, an' syne
he rade awa out o' sight, never comin' near the castle,
as Mauns thought he would hae done. ' Noo,' says
the baron till himsel', says he, ' I didna think that
there was ony ane in a' the land that could hae

played sic a ploy; but deil fetch me if I dinna lift it
as weel as he did !' Sae aff he gaed, for there wasna
sic a man for birr in a' the countra, an' he kent
it as weel, for he never met wi' his match. Weel,
he tried, and tugged, and better than tugged at the
stane, but he coudna mudge it ava; an' when he
looked about, he saw a man at his ilbuck, a' smeared
wi' smiddy-coom, snightern an' laughin' at him.
The laird d——d him, an' bade him lift it, whilk
he did as gin 't had been a little pinnin. The laird
was like to burst wi' rage at being fickled by sic a
hag-ma-hush carle, and he took to the stane in a
fury, and lifted it till his knee; but the weight o 't
amaist ground his banes to smash. He held the
stane till his een-strings crackit, when he was as
blin' as a moudiwort. He was blin' till the day o'
his death,—that 's to say, if ever he died, for there
were queer sayings about it—vera queer! vera queer!
The stane was ca'd Mauns' Stane ever after; an' it
was no thought that canny to be near it after gloaming; for what says the Psalm—hem!—I mean the
sang—

> 'Tween Ennetbutts an' Mauns' Stane
> Ilka night there walks ane !

" There never was a chief of the family after ; the
men were scattered, an' the castle demolished. The
doo and the hoodie-craw nestle i' their towers, and
the hare mak's her form on their grassy hearth-stane."

" Is this stone still to be seen ? "

"Ou, na. Ye see, it was just upon Johnie Forbes's craft, an' fouk cam' far an' near to leuk at it, an' trampit down a' the puir cottar-body's corn; sae he houkit a hole just aside it, and tumbled it intil 't; by that means naebody sees 't noo, but its weel kent that it 's there, for they 're livin' yet wha 've seen it."

"But the well at the Abbey—did no one feel a desire to enrich himself with the gold and silver buried there?"

"Hoot, ay; mony a ane tried to find out whaur it was, and, for that matter, I 've may be done as foolish a thing myself; but nane ever made it out. There was a scholar, like yoursel', that gaed ae night down to the Abbey, an', ye see, he summoned up the deil."

"The deuce he did!" said I.

"Weel, weel, the deuce, gin ye like it better," said he. "An' he was gaun to question him where the treasure was, but he had eneuch to do to get him laid without deaving him wi' questions, for a' the deils cam' about him, like bees biggin' out o' a byke. He never coured the fright he gat, but cried out, 'Help! help!' till his very enemy wad hae been wae to see him; and sae he cried till he died, which was no that lang after. Fouk sudna meddle wi' sic ploys!"

"Most wonderful! And do you believe that Beelzebub actually appeared to him?"

"Believe it! What for no?" said he, consequentially tapping the lid of his snuff-horn. "Didna my ain father see the evil ane i' the schule o' Auld Deer?"

"Indeed!"

"Weel, I wot he did that. A wheen idle callants, when the dominie was out at his twal'-hours, read the Lord's Prayer backlans, an' raised him, but couldna lay him again, for he threepit ower them that he wadna gang awa unless he gat ane o' them wi' him. Ye may be sure this put them in an awfu' swither. They were a' squallin' an' crawlin' and sprawlin' amo' the couples to get out o' his grips. Ane o' them gat out an' tauld the maister about it, an' when he cam' down, the melted lead was runnin' aff the roof o' the house wi' the heat, sae, flingin' to the black thief a young bit kittlen o' the schulemistress's, he sank through the floor wi' an awsome roar. I mysel' have heard the mistress misca'in her man about offering up the puir thing, baith saul and body, to Baal. But troth, I'm no clear to speak o' the like o' this at sic a time o' night; sae if your honour bena for another jug, I'll e'en wus you a gude-night, for it's wearin' late, an I maun awa' to Skippyfair i' the mornin'."

I assented to this, and quickly lost in sleep the remembrance of all these tales of the olden times.

"HORSE AND HATTOCK."

THE power of the fairies was not confined to
unchristened children alone; it was supposed frequently to be extended to full-grown people, especially such as in an unlucky hour were devoted to
the devil by the execrations of parents and of
masters; or those who were found asleep under a
rock, or on a green hill, belonging to the fairies, after
sunset, or, finally, to those who unwarily joined
their orgies. A tradition existed, during the seventeenth century, concerning an ancestor of the noble
family of Duffers, who, " walking abroad in the fields
near to his own house, was suddenly carried away,
and found the next day at Paris, in the French
king's cellar, with a silver cup in his hand. Being
brought into the king's presence, and questioned by
him who he was, and how he came thither, he told
his name, his country, and the place of his residence,
and that on such a day of the month, which proved
to be the day immediately preceding, being in the
fields, he heard a noise of a whirlwind, and of voices
crying ' Horse and hattock!' (this is the word which

the fairies are said to use when they remove from
any place), whereupon he cried 'Horse and hattock !'
also, and was immediately caught up and transported
through the air by the fairies to that place, where,
after he had drunk heartily, he fell asleep, and
before he woke the rest of the company were gone,
and had left him in the posture wherein he was
found. It is said the king gave him a cup which
was found in his hand, and dismissed him." The
narrator affirms "that the cup was still preserved,
and known by the name of the fairy cup." He adds
that Mr. Steward, tutor to the then Lord Duffers,
had informed him that, "when a boy at the school
of Forres, he and his school-fellows were once upon a
time whipping their tops in the churchyard, before
the door of the church, when, though the day was
calm, they heard a noise of a wind, and at some
distance saw the small dust begin to rise and turn
round, which motion continued advancing till it
came to the place where they were, whereupon they
began to bless themselves; but one of their number
being, it seems, a little more bold and confident
than his companion, said, 'Horse and hattock with
my top !' and immediately they all saw the top lifted
up from the ground, but could not see which way
it was carried, by reason of a cloud of dust which
was raised at the same time. They sought for
the top all about the place where it was taken
up, but in vain; and it was found afterwards in

the churchyard, on the other side of the church."
This legend is contained in a letter from a
learned gentleman in Scotland to Mr. Aubrey,
dated 15th March 1695, published in *Aubrey's
Miscellanies*.

SECRET COMMONWEALTH.

By MR. ROBERT KIRK, *Minister of Aberfoyle,* 1691.

THE Siths, or Fairies, they call *Sluagh Maith*, or the Goodpeople, it would seem, to prevent the dint of their ill attempts (for the Irish used to bless all they fear harm of), and are said to be of a middle nature betwixt man and angel, as were demons thought to be of old, of intelligent studious spirits, and light changeable bodies (like those called astral), somewhat of the nature of a condensed cloud, and best seen in twilight. These bodies be so pliable through the subtlety of the spirits that agitate them, that they can make them appear or disappear at pleasure. Some have bodies or vehicles so spongeous, thin, and defecat [pure] that they are fed by only sucking into some fine spirituous liquors, that pierce like pure air and oil; others feed more gross on the foyson [abundance] or substance of corn and liquors, or corn itself that grows on the surface of the earth, which these fairies steal away, partly invisible, partly preying on the grain, as do crows

154

and mice; wherefore in this same age they are sometimes heard to break bread, strike hammers, and to do such like services within the little hillocks they most do haunt; some whereof of old, before the Gospel dispelled Paganism, and in some bar- barous places as yet, enter houses after all are at rest, and set the kitchens in order, cleansing all the vessels.   Such drags go under the name of Brownies. When we have plenty, they have scarcity at their homes; and, on the contrary (for they are not em- powered to catch as much prey everywhere as they please), their robberies, notwithstanding, ofttimes occasion great ricks of corn not to bleed so well (as they call it), or prove so copious by very far as was expected by the owner.

Their bodies of congealed air are sometimes carried aloft, other whiles grovel in different shapes, and enter into any cranny or clift of the earth where air enters, to their ordinary dwellings; the earth being full of cavities and cells, and there being no place, no creature, but is supposed to have other animals (greater or lesser) living in or upon it as inhabitants; and no such thing as a pure wilderness in the whole universe.

We then (the more terrestrial kind have now so numerously planted all countries) do labour for that abstruse people, as well as for ourselves.   Albeit, when several countries were uninhabited by us, these had their easy tillage above ground, as we now. The print of those furrows do yet remain to be seen on the shoulders of very high hills, which was done when the campaign ground was wood and forest.

They remove to other lodgings at the beginning of each quarter of the year, so traversing till doomsday, being impotent of staying in one place, and finding some ease by so purning [journeying] and changing habitations. Their chameleon-like bodies swim in the air near the earth with bag and baggage; and at such revolution of time, seers, or men of the second sight (females being seldom so qualified) have very terrifying encounters with them, even on highways; who, therefore, awfully shun to travel abroad at these four seasons of the year, and thereby have made it a custom to this day among the Scottish-Irish to keep church duly every first Sunday of the quarter to *seun* or hallow themselves, their corn and cattle, from the shots and stealth of these wandering tribes; and many of these superstitious people will not be seen in church again till the next quarter begins, as if no duty were to be learnt or done by them, but all the use of worship and sermons were to save them from these arrows that fly in the dark.

They are distributed in tribes and orders, and have children, nurses, marriages, deaths, and burials in appearance, even as we (unless they so do for a mock-show, or to prognosticate some such things among us).

They are clearly seen by these men of the second sight to eat at funerals [and] banquets. Hence many of the Scottish-Irish will not taste meat at these meetings, lest they have communion with, or be poisoned by, them. So are they seen to carry the bier or coffin with the corpse among the middle-earth men to the grave. Some men of that exalted sight (whether by art or nature) have told me they have seen at these meetings a double man, or the shape of some man in two places; that is a super-terranean and a subterranean inhabitant, perfectly resembling one another in all points, whom he, not-withstanding, could easily distinguish one from another by some secret tokens and operations, and so go and speak to the man, his neighbour and familiar, passing by the apparition or resemblance of him. They avouch that every element and different state of being has animals resembling those of another element; as there be fishes sometimes at sea re-sembling monks of late order in all their hoods and dresses; so as the Roman invention of good and bad demons, and guardian angels particularly assigned, is called by them an ignorant mistake, sprung only from this original. They call this reflex man a co-walker, every way like the man, as a twin brother and companion, haunting him as his shadow, as is oft seen and known among men (resembling the original), both before and after the original is dead; and was often seen of old to enter a house, by which

the people knew that the person of that likeness
was to visit them within a few days.   This copy,
echo, or living picture, goes at last to his own herd.
It accompanied that person so long and frequently
for ends best known to itself, whether to guard him
from the secret assaults of some of its own folk, or
only as a sportful ape to counterfeit all his actions.
However, the stories of old witches prove beyond
contradiction that all sorts of people, spirits which
assume light airy bodies, or crazed bodies coacted
by foreign spirits, seem to have some pleasure (at
least to assuage some pain or melancholy) by frisk-
ing and capering like satyrs, or whistling and
screeching (like unlucky birds) in their unhallowed
synagogues and Sabbaths.   If invited and earnestly
required, these companions make themselves known
and familiar to men ; otherwise, being in a different
state and element, they neither can nor will easily
converse with them.   They avouch that a *heluo* or
great eater has a voracious elve to be his attender,
called a joint-eater or just-halver, feeding on the
pith and quintessence of what the man eats ; and
that, therefore, he continues lean like a hawk or
heron, notwithstanding his devouring appetite ; yet
it would seem they convey that substance elsewhere,
for these subterraneans eat but little in their dwellings, their food being exactly clean, and served up
by pleasant children, like enchanted puppets.
    Their houses are called large and fair, and (unless

at some odd occasions) unperceivable by vulgar eyes, like Rachland and other enchanted islands, having fir lights, continual lamps, and fires, often seen without fuel to sustain them. Women are yet alive who tell they were taken away when in child-bed to nurse fairy children, a lingering voracious image of them being left in their place (like their reflection in a mirror), which (as if it were some insatiable spirit in an assumed body) made first semblance to devour the meats that it cunningly carried by, and then left the carcass as if it expired and departed thence by a natural and common death. The child and fire, with food and all other necessaries, are set before the nurse how soon she enters, but she neither perceives any passage out, nor sees what those people do in other rooms of the lodging. When the child is weaned, the nurse dies, or is conveyed back, or gets it to her choice to stay there. But if any superterraneans be so subtle as to practise sleights for procuring the privacy to any of their mysteries (such as making use of their ointments, which, as Gyges' ring, make them invis-ible or nimble, or cast them in a trance, or alter their shape, or make things appear at a vast distance, etc.), they smite them without pain, as with a puff of wind, and bereave them of both the natural and acquired sights in the twinkling of an eye (both these sights, when once they come, being in the same organ and inseparable), or they strike them dumb. The tramontanes to this day place bread, the Bible, or a piece of iron, to save their women at such times from being thus stolen, and they commonly report that all uncouth, unknown wights are terrified by nothing earthly so much as cold iron. They deliver the reason to be that hell lying betwixt the chill tempests and the firebrands of scalding metals, and iron of the north (hence the loadstone causes a tendency to that point), by an antipathy thereto, these odious, far-scenting creatures shrug and fright at all that comes thence relating to so abhorred a place, whence their torment is either begun, or feared to come hereafter.

Their apparel and speech is like that of the people and country under which they live ; so are they seen to wear plaids and variegated garments in the Highlands of Scotland, and suanachs [plaids] therefore in Ireland. They speak but little, and that by way of whistling, clear, not rough. The very devils conjured in any country do answer in the language of the place ; yet sometimes the subterraneans speak more distinctly than at other times. Their women are said to spin very fine, to dye, to tossue, and embroider ; but whether it be as manual operation of substantial refined stuffs, with apt and solid instruments, or only curious cobwebs, unpalpable rainbows, and a phantastic imitation of the actions of more terrestrial mortals, since it transcended all the senses of the seer to discern whether, I leave to conjecture as I found it.

Their men travel much abroad, either presaging or aping the dismal and tragical actions of some amongst us; and have also many disastrous doings of their own, as convocations, fighting, gashes, wounds, and burials, both in the earth and air. They live much longer than we; yet die at last, or [at] least vanish from that state. 'Tis one of their tenets that nothing perisheth, but (as the sun and year) everything goes in a circle, lesser or greater, and is renewed and refreshed in its revolutions; as 'tis another, that every body in the creation moves (which is a sort of life); and that nothing moves but has another animal moving on it; and so on, to the utmost minutest corpuscle that's capable of being a receptacle of life.

They are said to have aristocratical rulers and laws, but no discernible religion, love, or devotion towards God, the blessed Maker of all: they disappear whenever they hear His name invoked, or the name of Jesus (at which all do bow willingly, or by constraint, that dwell above or beneath, within the earth), (Philip. ii. 10); nor can they act ought at that time after hearing of that sacred name. The Taiblsdear or seer, that corresponds with this kind of familiars, can bring them with a spell to appear to himself or others when he pleases, as readily as Endor Witch did those of her own

Scotch.

L

kind. He tells they are ever readiest to go on
hurtful errands, but seldom will be the messengers
of great good to men. He is not terrified with their
sight when he calls them, but seeing them in a surprise (as often as he does) frights him extremely,
and glad would he be quit of such, for the hideous
spectacles seen among them ; as the torturing of
some wight, earnest, ghostly, staring looks, skir-
mishes, and the like. They do not all the harm
which appearingly they have power to do ; nor are
they perceived to be in great pain, save that they
are usually silent and sullen. They are said to have
many pleasant toyish books; but the operation of
these pieces only appears in some paroxysms of
antic, corybantic jollity, as if ravished and prompted
by a new spirit entering into them at that instant,
lighter and merrier than their own. Other books
they have of involved, abstruse sense, much like the
Rosurcian [Rosicrucian] style. They have nothing
of the Bible, save collected parcels for charms and
counter-charms; not to defend themselves withal,
but to operate on other animals, for they are a
people invulnerable by our weapons, and albeit were-
wolves' and witches' true bodies are (by the union
of the spirit of nature that runs through all echoing
and doubling the blow towards another) wounded
at home, when the astral assumed bodies are
stricken elsewhere—as the strings of a second harp,
tuned to a unison, sound, though only one be

struck,—yet these people have not a second, or so gross a body at all, to be so pierced; but as air which when divided unites again; or if they feel pain by a blow, they are better physicians than we, and quickly cure. They are not subject to sore sicknesses, but dwindle and decay at a certain period, all about an age. Some say their continual sadness is because of their pendulous state (like those men, Luke xiii. 2-6), as uncertain what at the last revolution will become of them, when they are locked up into an unchangeable condition; and if they have any frolic fits of mirth, 'tis as the constrained grinning of a mort-head [death's-head], or rather as acted on a stage, and moved by another, ther [than?] cordially coming of themselves. But other men of the second sight, being illiterate, and unwary in their observations, learn from [differ from] those; one averring those subterranean people to be departed souls, attending a while in this inferior state, and clothed with bodies procured through their alms-deeds in this life; fluid, active, ethereal vehicles to hold them that they may not scatter nor wander, and be lost in the totum, or their first nothing; but if any were so impious as to have given no alms, they say, when the souls of such do depart, they sleep in an inactive state till they resume the terrestrial bodies again; others, that what the low-country Scotch call a wraith, and the Irish *taibhse*, or death's messenger (appearing some-

times as a little rough dog, and if crossed and conjured in time, will be pacified by the death of any
other creature instead of the sick man), is only
exuvious fumes of the man approaching death,
exhaled and congealed into a various likeness (as
ships and armies are sometimes shaped in the air),
and called astral bodies, agitated as wild-fire with
wind, and are neither souls nor counterfeiting
spirits; yet not a few avouch (as is said) that surely
these are a numerous people by themselves, having
their own politics, which diversities of judgment
may occasion several inconsonancies in this rehearsal,
after the narrowest scrutiny made about it.

Their weapons are most-what solid earthly
bodies, nothing of iron, but much of stone, like to
yellow soft flint spa, shaped like a barbed arrow-
head, but flung like a dart, with great force. These
arms (cut by art and tools, it seems, beyond human)
have somewhat of the nature of thunderbolt subtlety,
and mortally wounding the vital parts without
breaking the skin; of which wounds I have observed in beasts, and felt them with my hands.
They are not as infallible Benjamites, hitting at a
hair's-breadth; nor are they wholly unvanquishable,
at least in appearance.

The men of the second sight do not discover
strange things when asked, but at fits and raptures,
as if inspired with some genius at that instant,
which before did work in or about them. Thus I

have frequently spoken to one of them, who in his transport told me he cut the body of one of those people in two with his iron weapon, and so escaped this onset, yet he saw nothing left behind of that appearing divided; at other times he outwrested [wrestled?] some of them. His neighbours often perceived this man to disappear at a certain place, and about an hour after to become visible, and discover himself near a bow-shot from the first place. It was in that place where he became invisible, said he, that the subterraneans did encounter and combat with him. Those who are *unseund*, or unsanctified (called fey), are said to be pierced or wounded with those people's weapons, which makes them do somewhat very unlike their former practice, causing a sudden alteration, yet the cause thereof unperceivable at present; nor have they power (either they cannot make use of their natural powers, or asked not the heavenly aid) to escape the blow impendent. A man of the second sight perceived a person standing by him (sound to other's view) wholly gored in blood, and he (amazed like) bid him instantly flee. The whole man laughed at his *airt* [notice] and warning, since there was no appearance of danger. He had scarce contracted his lips from laughter when unexpectedly his enemies leaped in at his side and stabbed him with their weapons. They also pierce cows or other animals, usually said to be Elf-shot, whose purest substance (if they die) these subterraneans take to live on, viz. the aërial and ethereal parts, the most spirituous matter for prolonging of life, such as aquavitæ (moderately taken) is amongst liquors, leaving the terrestrial behind. The cure of such hurts is only for a man to find out the hole with his finger, as if the spirits flowing from a man's warm hand were antidote sufficient against their poisoned darts.

As birds, as beasts, whose bodies are much used to the change of the free and open air, foresee storms, so those invisible people are more sagacious to understand by the books of nature things to come, than we, who are pestered with the grossest dregs of all elementary mixtures, and have our purer spirits choked by them. The deer scents out a man and powder (though a late invention) at a great distance; a hungry hunter, bread; and the raven, a carrion; their brains, being long clarified by the high and subtle air, will observe a very small change in a trice. Thus a man of the second sight, perceiving the operations of these forecasting invisible people among us (indulged through a stupendous providence to give warnings of some remarkable events, either in the air, earth, or waters), told he saw a winding shroud creeping on a walking healthful person's leg till it came to the knee, and afterwards it came up to the middle, then to the shoulders, and at last over the head, which was visible to no other person. And by observing the spaces of time betwixt the several stages, he easily guessed how long the man was to live who wore the shroud; for when it approached the head, he told that such a person was ripe for the grave.

There be many places called fairy-hills, which the mountain people think impious and dangerous to peel or discover, by taking earth or wood from them, superstitiously believing the souls of their predecessors to dwell there. And for that end (say they) a mole or mound was dedicate beside every churchyard to receive the souls till their adjacent bodies arise, and so became as a fairy-hill; they using bodies of air when called abroad. They also affirm those creatures that move invisibly in a house, and cast huge great stones, but do no much hurt, because counter-wrought by some more courteous and charitable spirits that are everywhere ready to defend men (Dan. x. 13), to be souls that have not attained their rest, through a vehement desire of revealing a murder or notable injury done or received, or a treasure that was forgot in their life-time on earth, which, when disclosed to a conjuror alone, the ghost quite removes.

In the next country to that of my former residence, about the year 1676, when there was some scarcity of grain, a marvellous illapse and vision strongly struck the imagination of two women in one night, living at a good distance from one another, about a treasure hid in a hill called *Sith-bruthach*, or fairy-hill. The appearance of a treasure was first represented to the fancy, and then an audible voice named the place where it was to their awaking senses. Whereupon both rose, and meeting accidentally at the place, discovered their design; and jointly digging, found a vessel as large as a Scottish peck full of small pieces of good money, of ancient coin; and halving betwixt them, they sold in dish-fuls for dishfuls of meal to the country people. Very many of undoubted credit saw and had of the coin to this day. But whether it was a good or bad angel, one of the subterranean people, or the restless soul of him who hid it, that discovered it, and to what end it was done, I leave to the examination of others.

These subterraneans have controversies, doubts, disputes, feuds, and siding of parties; there being some ignorance in all creatures, and the vastest created intelligences not compassing all things. As to vice and sin, whatever their own laws be, sure according to ours, and equity, natural, civil, and revealed, they transgress and commit acts of injustice and sin by what is above said, as to their stealing of nurses to their children, and that other sort of plaginism in catching our children away (may seem to heir some estate in those invisible dominions) which never return. For swearing and intemper-ance, they are not observed so subject to those irregularities, as to envy, spite, hypocrisy, lying, and dissimulation.

As our religion obliges us not to make a peremptory and curious search into these abstrusenesses, so the histories of all ages give as many plain examples of extraordinary occurrences as make a modest inquiry not contemptible. How much is written of pigmies, fairies, nymphs, syrens, apparitions, which though not the tenth part true, yet could not spring of nothing; even English authors relate [of] Barry Island, in Glamorganshire, that laying your ear into a cleft of the rocks, blowing of bellows, striking of hammers, clashing of armour, filing of iron, will be heard distinctly ever since Merlin enchanted those subterranean wights to a solid manual forging of arms to Aurelius Ambrosius and his Britons, till he returned ; which Merlin being killed in a battle, and not coming to loose the knot, these active vulcans are there tied to a perpetual labour.

THE FAIRY BOY OF LEITH.

"About fifteen years since, having business that detained me for some time at Leith, which is near Edinburgh, in the kingdom of Scotland, I often met some of my acquaintance at a certain house there, where we used to drink a glass of wine for our refection. The woman which kept the house was of honest reputation among the neighbours, which made me give the more attention to what she told me one day about a fairy boy (as they called him) who lived about that town. She had given me so strange an account of him, that I desired her I might see him the first opportunity, which she promised; and not long after, passing that way, she told me there was the fairy boy, but a little before I came by; and, casting her eye into the street, said, 'Look you, sir, yonder he is, at play with those other boys'; and pointing him out to me, I went, and by smooth words, and a piece of money, got him to come into the house with me; where, in the presence of divers people, I demanded of him several astrological questions, which he answered

with great subtlety ; and, through all his discourse,
carried it with a cunning much above his years,
which seemed not to exceed ten or eleven.

"He seemed to make a motion like drumming upon
the table with his fingers, upon which I asked him
whether he could beat a drum? To which he replied, 'Yes, sir, as well as any man in Scotland ;
for every Thursday night I beat all points to a sort of
people that used to meet under yonder hill' (pointing to the great hill between Edinburgh and Leith).
'How, boy?' quoth I, 'what company have you
there ?' 'There are, sir,' said he, 'a great company
both of men and women, and they are entertained
with many sorts of music besides my drum ; they
have, besides, plenty of variety of meats and wine,
and many times we are carried into France or
Holland in the night, and return again, and whilst
we are there, we enjoy all the pleasures the country
doth afford.' I demanded of him how they got
under that hill? To which he replied that there
was a great pair of gates that opened to them,
though they were invisible to others, and that
within there were brave large rooms, as well ac-
commodated as most in Scotland. I then asked
him how I should know what he said to be true?
Upon which he told me he would read my fortune,
saying, I should have two wives, and that he saw
the forms of them over my shoulders ; and both
would be very handsome women.

The woman of the house told me that all the people in Scotland could not keep him from the rendezvous on Thursday night; upon which, by promising him some more money, I got a promise of him to meet me at the same place in the afternoon, the Thursday following, and so dismissed him at that time. The boy came again at the place and time appointed, and I had prevailed with some friends to continue with me (if possible) to prevent his moving that night. He was placed between us, and answered many questions, until, about eleven of the clock, he was got away unperceived by the company; but I, suddenly missing him, hastened to the door, and took hold of him, and so returned him into the same room. We all watched him, and, of a sudden, he was again got out of doors; I followed him close, and he made a noise in the street, as if he had been set upon, and from that time I could never see him."

THE DRACÆ.

THESE are a sort of water-spirits who inveigle women and children into the recesses which they inhabit, beneath lakes and rivers, by floating past them, on the surface of the water, in the shape of gold rings or cups. The women thus seized are employed as nurses, and after seven years are permitted to revisit earth. Gervase mentions one woman in particular who had been allured by observing a wooden dish, or cup, float'by her, while she was washing clothes in the river. Being seized as soon as she reached the depths, she was conducted into one of the subterranean recesses, which she described as very magnificent, and employed as nurse to one of the brood of the hag who had allured her. During her residence in this capacity, having accidentally touched one of her eyes with an ointment of serpent's grease, she perceived, at her return to the world, that she had acquired the faculty of seeing the *Dracæ*, when they intermingle themselves with men. Of this power she was, however, deprived by the touch of her ghostly mistress,

whom she had one day incautiously addressed. It
is a curious fact that this story, in almost all its
parts, is current in both the Highlands and Low-
lands of Scotland, with no other variation than
the substitution of Fairies for Dracæ, and the
cavern of a hill for that of a river. Indeed many
of the vulgar account it extremely dangerous to
touch anything which they may happen to find
without saining (blessing) it, the snares of the
enemy being notorious and well-attested. A poor
woman of Teviotdale having been fortunate enough,
as she thought herself, to find a wooden beetle, at
the very time when she needed such an implement,
seized it without pronouncing a proper blessing, and,
carrying it home, laid it above her bed to be ready
for employment in the morning. At midnight the
window of her cottage opened, and a loud voice was
heard calling up some one within by a strange and
uncouth name. The terrified cottager ejaculated a
prayer, which, we may suppose, ensured her personal
safety; while the enchanted implement of house-
wifery, tumbling from the bedstead, departed by the
window with no small noise and precipitation. In
a humorous fugitive tract, Dr. Johnson has been
introduced as disputing the authenticity of an
apparition, merely because the spirit assumed the
shape of a teapot and a shoulder of mutton. No
doubt, a case so much in point as that we have now
quoted would have removed his incredulity.

A SUCCINCT ACCOUNT

OF

MY LORD TARBAT'S RELATIONS,

IN A LETTER TO THE HONORABLE ROBERT BOYLE, ESQUIRE, OF THE PREDICTIONS MADE BY SEERS, WHEREOF HIMSELF WAS EAR- AND EYE-WITNESS.

SIR,—I heard very much, but believed very little of the second sight; yet its being assumed by several of great veracity, I was induced to make inquiry after it in the year 1652, being then confined in the north of Scotland by the English usurpers. The more general accounts of it were that many Highlanders, yet far more Islanders, were qualified with this second sight; and men, women, and children, indistinctly, were subject to it, and children where parents were not. Sometimes people came to age who had it not when young, nor could any tell by what means produced. It is a trouble to most of them who are subject to it, and they would be rid of it at any rate if they could. The sight is of no

long duration, only continuing so long as they can
keep their eyes steady without twinkling. The
hardy, therefore, fix their look that they may see
the longer; but the timorous see only glances—their
eyes always twinkle at the first sight of the object.
That which generally is seen by them are the species
of living creatures, and of inanimate things, which
be in motion, such as ships, and habits upon persons. They never see the species of any person
who is already dead. What they foresee fails not
to exist in the mode, and in that place where it
appears to them. They cannot well know what
space of time shall intervene between the apparition
and the real existence. But some of the hardiest
and longest experience have some rules for conjec-
tures; as, if they see a man with a shrouding sheet
in the apparition, they will conjecture at the near-
ness or remoteness of his death by the more or less
of his body that is covered by it. They will ordinarily see their absent friends, though at a great
distance, sometimes no less than from America to
Scotland, sitting, standing, or walking in some certain place; and then they conclude with an assurance that they will see them so, and there. If a man
be in love with a woman, they will ordinarily see
the species of that man standing by her, and so likewise if a woman be in love. If they see the species
of any person who is sick to die, they see them
covered over with the shrouding sheet.

These generals I had verified to me by such of
them as did see, and were esteemed honest and
sober by all the neighbourhood ; for I inquired after
such for my information. And because there were
more of these seers in the isles of Lewis, Harris,
and Uist than in any other place, I did entreat Sir
James M'Donald (who is now dead), Sir Normand
M'Loud, and Mr. Daniel Morison, a very honest
person (who are still alive), to make inquiry in this
uncouth sight, and to acquaint me therewith; which
they did, and all found an agreement in these generals, and informed me of many instances confirming
what they said. But though men of discretion and
honour, being but at second-hand, I will choose
rather to put myself than my friends on the hazard
of being laughed at for incredible relations.

I was once travelling in the Highlands, and a
good number of servants with me, as is usual there;
and one of them, going a little before me, entering
into a house where I was to stay all night, and going
hastily to the door, he suddenly slipped back with a
screech, and did fall by a stone, which hit his foot.
I asked what the matter was, for he seemed to be
very much frighted. He told me very seriously that
I should not lodge in that house, because shortly a
dead coffin would be carried out of it, for many were
carrying of it when he was heard cry. I, neglecting
his words, and staying there, he said to other of his
servants he was sorry for it, and that surely what

Scotch.

M

he saw would shortly come to pass. Though no sick person was then there, yet the landlord, a healthy Highlander, died of an apoplectic fit before I left the house.

In the year 1653 Alexander Monro (afterwards Lieutenant-Colonel to the Earl of Dumbarton's regiment) and I were walking in a place called Ullapool, in Loch Broom, on a little plain at the foot of a rugged hill. There was a servant walking with a spade in the walk before us; his back was to us, and his face to the hill. Before we came to him he let the spade fall, and looked toward the hill. He took notice of us as we passed near by him, which made me look at him, and perceiving him to stare a little strangely I conjectured him to be a seer. I called at him, at which he started and smiled. "What are you doing?" said I. He answered, "I have seen a very strange thing: an army of Englishmen, leading of horses, coming down that hill; and a number of them are coming down to the plain, and eating the barley which is growing in the field near to the hill." This was on the 4th May (for I noted the day), and it was four or five days before the barley was sown in the field he spoke of. Alexander Monro asked him how he knew they were Englishmen. He said because they were leading of horses, and had on hats and boots, which he knew no Scotchman would have there. We took little notice of the whole story as other than a foolish vision, but wished that an English party were there, we being then at war with them, and the place almost inaccessible for horsemen. But in the beginning of August thereafter, the Earl of Middleton (then Lieutenant for the King in the Highlands), having occasion to march a party of his towards the South Highlands, he sent his Foot through a place called Inverlawell; and the fore-party, which was first down the hill, did fall off eating the barley which was on the little plain under it. And Monro calling to mind what the seer told us in May preceding, he wrote of it, and sent an express to me to Lochslin, in Ross (where I then was), with it.

I had occasion once to be in company where a young lady was (excuse my not naming of persons), and I was told there was a notable seer in the company. I called him to speak with me, as I did ordinarily when I found any of them; and after he had answered me several questions, I asked if he knew any person to be in love with that lady. He said he did, but he knew not the person; for, during the two days he had been in her company, he perceived one standing near her, and his head leaning on her shoulder, which he said did foretell that the man should marry her, and die before her, according to his observation. This was in the year 1655. I desired him to describe the person, which he did, so that I could conjecture, by the description, of such a one, who was of that lady's acquaintance, though there were no thoughts of their marriage till two years thereafter. And having occasion in the year 1657 to find this seer, who was an islander, in company with the other person whom I conjectured to have been described by him, I called him aside, and asked if that was the person he saw beside the lady near two years then past. He said it was he indeed, for he had seen that lady just then standing by him hand in hand. This was some few months before their marriage, and that man is now dead, and the lady alive.

I shall trouble you but with one more, which I thought most remarkable of any that occurred to me.

In January 1652, the above-mentioned Lieutenant, Colonel Alex. Monro, and I, happened to be in the house of one William M'Clend, of Ferrinlea, in the county of Ross. He, the landlord, and I, were sitting in three chairs near the fire, and in the corner of the great chimney there were two islanders, who were that very night come to the house, and were related to the landlord. While the one of them was talking with Monro, I perceived the other to look oddly toward me. From this look, and his being an islander, I conjectured him a seer, and asked him at what he stared. He answered by desiring me to rise from that chair, for it was an unlucky one. I asked him why? He answered, because there was a dead man in the chair next to me. "Well," said I, "if it be in the next chair, I may keep my own. But what is the likeness of the man?" He said he was a tall man, with a long grey coat, booted, and one of his legs hanging over the arm of the chair, and his head hanging dead to the other side, and his arm backward, as if it was broken. There were some English troops then quartered near that place, and there being at that time a great frost after a thaw, the country was covered all over with ice. Four or five of the English riding by this house some two hours after the vision, while we were sitting by the fire, we heard a great noise, which proved to be those troopers, with the help of other servants, carrying in one of their number, who had got a very mischievous fall, and had his arm broke; and falling frequently in swooning fits, they brought him into the hall, and set him in the very chair, and in the very posture that the seer had prophesied. But the man did not die, though he recovered with great difficulty.

Among the accounts given me by Sir Normand M'Loud, there was one worthy of special notice, which was thus:—There was a gentleman in the Isle of Harris, who was always seen by the seers with an arrow in his thigh. Such in the Isle who thought those prognostications infallible, did not doubt but he would be shot in the thigh before he died. Sir Normand told me that he heard it the

subject of their discourse for many years.   At last
he died without any such accident.   Sir Normand
was at his burial at St. Clement's Church in the
Harris.   At the same time the corpse of another
gentleman was brought to be buried in the same
very church.   The friends on either side came to
debate who should first enter the church, and, in a
trice, from words they came to blows.   One of the
number (who was armed with bow and arrows) let
one fly among them.   (Now every family in that
Isle have their burial-place in the Church in stone
chests, and the bodies are carried in open biers to
the burial-place.)   Sir Normand having appeased the
tumult, one of the arrows was found shot in the dead
man's thigh.   To this Sir Normand was a witness.

In the account which Mr. Daniel Morison, parson
in the Lewis, gave me, there was one, though it be
heterogeneous from the subject, yet it may be worth
your notice.   It was of a young woman in this
parish, who was mightily frightened by seeing her
own image still before her, always when she came
to the open air; the back of the image being always
to her, so that it was not a reflection as in a mirror,
but the species of such a body as her own, and in a
very like habit which appeared to herself continually
before her.   The parson kept her a long while with
him, but had no remedy of her evil, which troubled
her exceedingly.   I was told afterwards that when
she was four or five years older she saw it not.

These are matters of fact, which I assure you they are truly related. But these and all others that occurred to me, by information or otherwise, could never lead me into a remote conjecture of the cause of so extraordinary a phenomenon. Whether it be a quality in the eyes of some people in these parts, concurring with a quality in the air also; whether such species be everywhere, though not seen by the want of eyes so qualified, or from whatever other cause, I must leave to the inquiry of clearer judgments than mine. But a hint may be taken from this image which appeared still to this woman above mentioned, and from another mentioned by Aristotle, in the fourth of his Metaphysics (if I remember right, for it is long since I read it), as also from the common opinion that young infants (unsullied with many objects) do see apparitions which were not seen by those of elder years ; as likewise from this, that several did see the second sight when in the Highlands or Isles, yet when transported to live in other countries, especially in America, they quite lose this quality, as was told me by a gentleman who knew some of them in Barbadoes, who did see no vision there, although he knew them to be seers when they lived in the Isles of Scotland.

Thus far my Lord Tarbat.

THE BOGLE.

THIS is a freakish spirit who delights rather to perplex and frighten mankind than either to serve or seriously hurt them. The *Esprit Follet* of the French, Shakespeare's Puck, or Robin Goodfellow, and Shellycoat, a spirit who resides in the waters, and has given his name to many a rock and stone on the Scottish coast, belong to the class of bogles. One of Shellycoat's pranks is thus narrated :—Two men in a very dark night, approaching the banks of the Ettrick, heard a doleful voice from its waves repeatedly exclaim, "Lost ! lost !" They followed the sound, which seemed to be the voice of a drowning person, and, to their astonishment, found that it ascended the river ; still they continued to follow the cry of the malicious sprite, and, arriving before dawn at the very sources of the river, the voice was now heard descending the opposite side of the mountain in which they arise. The fatigued and deluded travellers now relinquished the pursuit, and had no sooner done so, than they heard Shellycoat applauding, in loud bursts of laughter, his successful roguery

DAOINE SHIE, OR THE MEN OF PEACE.

THEY are, though not absolutely malevolent, believed to be a peevish, repining, and envious race, who enjoy, in the subterranean recesses, a kind of shadowy splendour. The Highlanders are at all times unwilling to speak of them, but especially on Friday, when their influence is supposed to be particularly extensive. As they are supposed to be invisibly present, they are at all times to be spoken of with respect. The fairies of Scotland are represented as a diminutive race of beings, of a mixed or rather dubious nature, capricious in their dispositions, and mischievous in their resentment. They inhabit the interior of green hills, chiefly those of a conical form, in Gaelic termed *Sighan*, on which they lead their dances by moonlight, impressing upon the surface the marks of circles, which sometimes appear yellow and blasted, sometimes of a deep green hue, and within which it is dangerous to sleep, or to be found after sunset. The removal of those large portions of turf, which thunderbolts sometimes scoop out of the ground with singular regularity, is also ascribed to their agency. Cattle which are suddenly seized with the cramp, or some similar disorder, are said to be elf-shot, and the approved cure is to chafe the parts affected with a blue bonnet, which, it may be readily believed, often restores the circulation. The triangular flints frequently found in Scotland, with which the ancient inhabitants probably barbed their shafts, are supposed to be the weapons of fairy resentment, and are termed elf arrowheads. The rude brazen battle-axes of the ancients, commonly called " celts," are also ascribed to their manufacture. But, like the Gothic duergar, their skill is not confined to the fabrication of arms; for they are heard sedulously hammering in linns, precipices, and rocky or cavernous situations, where, like the dwarfs of the mines mentioned by George Agricola, they busy themselves in imitating the actions and the various employments of men. The Brook of Beaumont, for example, which passes in its course by numerous linns and caverns, is notorious for being haunted by the fairies; and the perforated and rounded stones which are formed by trituration in its channels are termed by the vulgar fairy cups and dishes. A beautiful reason is assigned by Fletcher for the fays frequenting streams and fountains. He tells us of

> " A virtuous well, about whose flowery banks
> The nimble-footed fairies dance their rounds
> By the pale moonshine, dipping oftentimes
> Their stolen children, so to make them free
> From dying flesh and dull mortality."

.

It is sometimes accounted unlucky to pass such
places without performing some ceremony to avert
the displeasure of the elves. There is upon the top
of Minchmuir, a mountain in Peeblesshire, a spring
called the Cheese Well, because, anciently, those
who passed that way were wont to throw into it a
piece of cheese as an offering to the fairies, to whom
it was consecrated.

Like the *feld elfen* of the Saxons, the usual dress
of the fairies is green ; though, on the moors, they
have been sometimes observed in heath-brown, or in
weeds dyed with the stone-raw or lichen. They
often ride in invisible procession, when their presence
is discovered by the shrill ringing of their bridles.
On these occasions they sometimes borrow mortal
steeds, and when such are found at morning, panting
and fatigued in their stalls, with their manes and
tails dishevelled and entangled, the grooms, I presume, often find this a convenient excuse for their
situation, as the common belief of the elves quaffing
the choicest liquors in the cellars of the rich might
occasionally cloak the delinquencies of an unfaithful
butler.

The fairies, besides their equestrian processions,
are addicted, it would seem, to the pleasures of the
chase. A young sailor, travelling by night from
Douglas, in the Isle of Man, to visit his sister residing in Kirk Merlugh, heard a noise of horses, the
holloa of a huntsman, and the sound of a horn.

Immediately afterwards, thirteen horsemen, dressed in green, and gallantly mounted, swept past him. Jack was so much delighted with the sport that he followed them, and enjoyed the sound of the horn for some miles, and it was not till he arrived at his sister's house that he learned the danger which he had incurred. I must not omit to mention that these little personages are expert jockeys, and scorn to ride the little Manx ponies, though apparently well suited to their size. The exercise, therefore, falls heavily upon the English and Irish horses brought into the Isle of Man. Mr. Waldron was assured by a gentleman of Ballafletcher that he had lost three or four capital hunters by these nocturnal excursions. From the same author we learn that the fairies sometimes take more legitimate modes of procuring horses. A person of the utmost integrity informed him that, having occasion to sell a horse, he was accosted among the mountains by a little gentleman plainly dressed, who priced his horse, cheapened him, and, after some chaffering, finally purchased him. No sooner had the buyer mounted and paid the price than he sank through the earth, horse and man, to the astonishment and terror of the seller, who experienced, however, no inconvenience from dealing with so extraordinary a purchaser.

THE DEATH "BREE."

THERE was once a woman, who lived in the Camp-del-more of Strathavon, whose cattle were seized with a murrain, or some such fell disease, which ravaged the neighbourhood at the time, carrying off great numbers of them daily. All the forlorn fires and hallowed waters failed of their customary effects; and she was at length told by the wise people, whom she consulted on the occasion, that it was evidently the effect of some infernal agency, the power of which could not be destroyed by any other means than the never-failing specific—the juice of a dead head from the churchyard,—a nostrum certainly very difficult to be procured, considering that the head must needs be abstracted from the grave at the hour of midnight. Being, however, a woman of a stout heart and strong faith, native feelings of delicacy towards the sanctuary of the dead had more weight than had fear in restraining her for some time from resorting to this desperate remedy. At length, seeing that her stock would soon be annihilated by the destructive career of the disease, the wife of Camp-del-more resolved to put the experiment in practice, whatever the result might be. Accordingly, having with considerable difficulty engaged a neighbouring woman as her companion in this hazardous expedition, they set out a little before midnight for the parish churchyard, distant about a mile and a half from her residence, to execute her determination. On arriving at the churchyard her companion, whose courage was not so notable, appalled by the gloomy prospect before her, refused to enter among the habitations of the dead. She, however, agreed to remain at the gate till her friend's business was accomplished. This circumstance, however, did not stagger the wife's resolution. She, with the greatest coolness and intrepidity, proceeded towards what she supposed an old grave, took down her spade, and commenced her operations. After a good deal of toil she arrived at the object of her labour. Raising the first head, or rather skull, that came in her way, she was about to make it her own property, when a hollow, wild, sepulchral voice exclaimed, "That is my head; let it alone!" Not wishing to dispute the claimant's title to this head, and supposing she could be otherwise provided, she very good-naturedly returned it and took up another. "That is my father's head," bellowed the same voice. Wishing, if possible, to avoid disputes, the wife of Camp-del-more took up another head, when the

same voice instantly started a claim to it as his
grandfather's head. "Well," replied the wife,
nettled at her disappointments, "although it were
your grandmother's head, you shan't get it till I am
done with it." "What do you say, you limmer?"
says the ghost, starting up in his awry habiliments.
"What do you say, you limmer?" repeated he in a
great rage. "By the great oath, you had better
leave my grandfather's head." Upon matters coming
this length, the wily wife of Camp-del-more thought
it proper to assume a more conciliatory aspect.
Telling the claimant the whole particulars of the
predicament in which she was placed, she promised
faithfully that if his honour would only allow her
to carry off his grandfather's skull or head in a
peaceable manner, she would restore it again when
done with. Here, after some communing, they
came to an understanding; and she was allowed to
take the head along with her, on condition that she
should restore it before cock-crowing, under the
heaviest penalties.

On coming out of the churchyard and looking
for her companion, she had the mortification to find
her "without a mouthful of breath in her body";
for, on hearing the dispute between her friend and
the guardian of the grave, and suspecting much
that she was likely to share the unpleasant punish-
ments with which he threatened her friend, at the
bare recital of them she fell down in a faint, from

which it was no easy matter to recover her. This proved no small inconvenience to Camp-del-more's wife, as there were not above two hours to elapse ere she had to return the head according to the terms of her agreement. Taking her friend upon her back, she carried her up a steep acclivity to the nearest adjoining house, where she left her for the night; then repaired home with the utmost speed, made *dead bree* of the head ere the appointed time had expired, restored the skull to its guardian, and placed the grave in its former condition. It is needless to add that, as a reward for her exemplary courage, the "*bree*" had its desired effect. The cattle speedily recovered, and, so long as she retained any of it, all sorts of diseases were of short duration.

Printed by T. and A. CONSTABLE, Printers to Her Majesty, *at the Edinburgh University Press.*

www.ingramcontent.com/pod-product-compliance
Lightning Source LLC
Chambersburg PA
CBHW030834270326
41928CB00007B/1048